SHANE MITCHELL

THE
CROP
CYCLE

STORIES WITH DEEP ROOTS

BS
publishing

THE CROP CYCLE
STORIES WITH DEEP ROOTS

Published by The Bitter Southerner, Inc.
Athens, Georgia

ISBN: 978-0-9980293-1-3

Front Cover:
Tomato illustration by Courtney Garvin
Cover design by Dave Whitling

Designed in the South.
Printed in Canada.

FOR THE AUNTSISTERS

"HELP YOURSELF."

—

LYDIA ALTA ANDERSON MITCHELL

CONTENTS

INTRODUCTION

The Crop Cycle **began with a one-liner.** "I hate grits." That was it, the family joke about a girl with Southern roots who wasn't always enamored by them. And it launched a years-long saga—tromping around fields on heat stroke days, dodging snakes and gators, salving fire ant and mosquito bites, learning to spot century plants as markers for labor camps and crying in cars after visiting broken down trailer homes, being welcomed into kitchens for a hot meal, being sent away with a bundle of okra, a jar of pickles, a paper bag of ripe-to-bursting tomatoes. Roadside stands. Pick your own. Parades. Pageants. Marches, rallies, and protests. Church as sanctuary, music as church. Scary flags, scary tattoos, scary histories. Being told not to come around anymore, being invited back anytime. Up at dawn with farmers, lurking in ag labs with botanists and horticulturalists. A road trip playlist with George Gershwin, Guy Clarke, RZA, Prince, Aretha Franklin, The Allman Brothers, The Presidents of the United States of America, Ashford & Simpson, Dr. John, The Rolling Stones. (Hint: They all sang about food.) Far too many Waffle House breakfast specials and fill-ups at Buc-ee's. (While not excusing the chain's disgraceful track record of employee relations or the hatejacking of its bucktoothed beaver by extremists, once or twice I almost ran out of gas and coasted in on fumes.) But also empanadas, boudin, kolaches, lumpia, vada pav, nieves, po'boys, lemon pepper wet wings, pulled pork, peach cobbler, Frito pie, and yes, my old nemesis, grits.

At heart, *The Crop Cycle* is not about food, but how we center it as a way to understand cycles of life. Each story, here in chronological order from that first one on grits in 2015, paid respects to many of my own family, although sadly not all, and took me in unexpected directions, from the Fogg Museum at Harvard to Talladega Superspeedway in Alabama. As detours go, this was leading down tobacco road. Because while you may not eat it, you sure can chew it. Even so, I spent considerable harvests gathering whatever is both bountiful and terrible about the place we all simply call The South.

—Shane Mitchell

Photo by Fernando Decillis

11

Nominated, James Beard Foundation's
Food and Culture Journalism Award, 2016

KISS MY
GRITS

"Eat your grits."

"No."

"Don't you know?" my mother asked. "There are children starving in Africa."

"Not my problem."

"We don't let food go to waste in this house, young lady, so you will sit there until every bite is gone."

My mother, a beautiful redhead from Florence, South Carolina, knew this was an empty threat. We'd been at this kitchen table standoff over boiled-corn particulate before. Left on the plate long enough to congeal, either by accident or picky-eater pigheadedness, the breakfast bane of my childhood took on a disgusting texture: lumpy on top with a slimy underside like the exposed white belly of a dead snake flattened on the road. It made me gag, but there was a certain perverse pleasure to poking it with a fork.

I hate grits.

Buzzard poo. Spackling paste. Corpse skin.

As a cultural marker, this one sticks to the ribs of the region, so much that the states sandwiched between Texas and Virginia have been christened "The Grits Belt." Charleston's paper of record, *The Post and Courier*, proclaimed in 1952 that grits were a "thoroughly digestible food." Georgia declared grits its official prepared food in

2002. In *Good Old Grits*, North Carolina chef and author Bill Neal wrote: "On every breakfast plate in the South there always appears a little white mound of food. Sometimes it's ignored. Sometimes insulted. But without it, the sun wouldn't come up, the crops wouldn't grow, and most of us would lose our drawl."

Despite this geographic ubiquity, all grits aren't good. I discovered that my distaste might have more to do with an inventor from Crystal Lake, Illinois, than my parent's stovetop skills.

Instant grits probably seemed like a good idea at the time. If you were raised in a Southern family during the 1970s, a man named Roy G. Hyldon was largely responsible for what wound up being served at breakfast. Postwar convenience foods still dominated supermarket shelves; "heirloom" referred to your Nana's silver service; even brilliant cooks like my mother occasionally defaulted to a cardboard container emblazoned with the logo of a bewigged religious elder.

In 1967, Hyldon and his associate James T. Collins filed US Patent 3,526,512 for perfecting "an instant food product of the corn grits type" for the Quaker Oats Company. The process as defined in the patent description involved admixing corn grits with polysaccharide gum and emulsifiers in order to create a product that can be prepared "by the mere addition of warm water . . . in a serving bowl."

Buried in the patent's technical lingo about "dried sheets of discrete particles in a starch matrix" is this unappetizing paragraph:

"When conventional corn grits are prepared in large quantities and stored on a steam table or the like to keep them warm until serving, they soon become an adhesive mass or cake and lose the texture associated with grits. Our new process, however, has provided us with a corn grits product wherein the forming of an adhesive mass or cake is postponed several hours. This results in a product which retains the grits' texture for the longest of normal serving times for the product."

What a depressing triumph of science over taste.

JIM CRACK CORN

"I've got to move all this by end of the day," Greg Johnsman said, dodging around 50-pound sacks of food-grade yellow dent corn piled atop pallets in his storage barn at Geechie Boy Market & Mill on South Carolina's Edisto Island. Johnsman's operation was a few miles over the McKinley Washington Jr. Bridge, which replaced the old swing bridge in 1993.

A heavyset man with impressive facial hair, the curlicue "Grits" logo on his T-shirt was dusted with meal. We were inspecting his collection of vintage milling and farm equipment. A Gibbs Machinery Company grits separator. A 1953 John Deere tractor. A seed cleaner picked up from an academic studying peas in Georgia. An early Meadows grits bolter, which has the serial number 382 hand-stenciled on its wooden casing—only 600 were built before the company shifted to metal housings in the 1920s. Johnsman flipped open the lid and pointed to a smudged signature. Neither of us could decipher the name, but the pencil script reads "Edisto Island" underneath.

Edisto was my family's home ground. They have lived on this sea island for more than 325 years, through wars, pestilence, hurricanes, crop failure, and real estate development. My father and brother were named for the place. My grandparents, childhood sweethearts and second cousins, crossed over the water because New York called, and would never return to the island permanently. Well, except after life. He died unexpectedly, far too young, leaving Nana and their three little sons devastated, at the end of the Great Depression and on the cusp of a world war.

Years later, on summer visits, Nana hauled me around to pay social calls in stuffy front parlors of plantation houses belonging to her cousins. Most mornings, some elderly relative's lumpy grits were served at breakfast and impolitely declined by an obstinate child with no discernable table manners whatsoever. Now, I go back to sweep family headstones in the island cemetery plot, inhale the iodine scent of pluff mud at low tide, and eat boiled peanuts. If you're thinking, how can she like slimy peanuts but not slimy grits? Don't be a jackass.

. . .

While Johnsman's field hands unloaded collards from a flatbed truck parked in the cleaning shed, his wife Betsy fielded orders from restaurants, and their 5-year-old son Victor dragged me by the hand to show off his baby chicks in a cardboard box. They were nearly the same sunny shade as freshly ground corn heaped in the climate-controlled milling room.

"I've never bought a new mill," Johnsman shouted as the belt drive whirred on his mid-century separator. "Don't know what that's like. The old equipment turns at 600 rpm. The new equipment turns at 1,800 rpm." He stuck a scoop of grits under my nose. "The beauty of all this old equipment is that slow speed does not generate much heat and leaves the corn in its most natural state. If I mill corn right out of the field, that's cooking it. Here in the Deep South? This is the worse place in the world to mill with the humidity and everything."

Cracking corn was an ancient technique. Before mechanized mills, there were metate or hand querns. The early Mayans boiled maize in an alkaline solution of water and lime, which softened the hull and made the kernels easier to grind, transforming it into a more nutritious substance known as nixtamal. The Native American word hominy defines the same process but leads to a sticky semantics side issue, so for now, let's skip to what happened when Americans first introduced wind- and water-driven mills. George Washington owned a profitable gristmill at Mount Vernon. Thomas Jefferson built two along the Rivanna River near Monticello. In 1790, the newly inaugurated US Patent Office granted inventor George Evans Patent 3 for his automated milling technology. From there to Hyldon's Patent 3,526,512 is a matter of 177 years and several left turns in Southern breakfast history.

...

Greg Johnsman's separator fell somewhere in between on this timeline, before small mills became obsolete in rural Southern communities. When forced between his mill's bed and runner stones, the corn kernels were cracked, then sifted through screens as bran was skimmed off. The grind was adjusted depending on the orders Johnsman needed to fill. His grits had caught on beyond the Belt.

"We can create all cornmeal or all chicken feed," he said. "But our business is making grits, so we have to find a common balance." He pointed to a crate of stitch-sealed paper sacks. "That's some Jimmy Red we just milled." He grabbed up a bag of this heirloom variety and offered it to me.

At his roadside market next to the mill, the two of us chugged bottles of Cheerwine from the cooler and continued the history lesson. Above our heads hung a battered wooden scoop.

"That looks insignificant, but it's one of the most special pieces I have. A miller said to me: 'Son, this is the money.' Families brought in their corn and got the meal back. But the miller would take one scoop out of your bag and set it to the side. Then he would sell it to doctors and lawyers in town. So that's a tariff scoop. It's not a standard measurement, but it's how he made a living."

In the corner, behind piles of fresh vegetables from the farm, sat a 1945 mill and separator he promised to put on display after buying it from a retired miller in Saluda, North Carolina. He pointed to an innocuous nail on one side below the meal screener.

"You see that nail?" he asked. "It took me two years to figure out what it was for. Someone prior to me found a shortcut. By adding that one nail was how he could hold a bag properly and improve the product process drastically.

"There's no miller store, no technical school; milling was just taught and passed on from whatever benefited each person," he said. "So when I find these little nuances, I kind of get to hold hands with a gentleman who came before me."

I examined an inscription Johnsman hand-lettered in black on the mill's wood casing: High Speed Chicken Feed.

"At the time, I thought it had to do with corn," he said. "Someone had to tell me it's trucker slang for uppers."

JIMMY RED

"Yaller is for critters," Glenn Roberts said.

If Johnsman was miller and farmer, then Roberts was miller and missionary. The founder of Anson Mills was bent on cornering market share of antebellum identity crops. He succeeded for a while. In an outbuilding at Clemson's Coastal Research and Education Center (CREC), a few miles south of Charleston on Savannah Highway and directly across from the seed vaults at the US Vegetable Lab, we looked at a kernel of Jimmy Red under a magnifying glass. "If you grew up South of Broad in Charleston, you'd never eat anything but white grits," he said. Upcountry and farther along the frontier, he claimed, people couldn't afford to be as picky about the color of their breakfast cereal.

Just in from the fields where late fall crops were still being tended, Dr. Brian Ward held up the Jimmy Red kernel and identified components: pericarp, endosperm, germ, tipcap. A vegetable specialist in charge of the Organic Research Farm, he wore khaki shorts, mud-scuffed work boots, and a checked shirt bearing the university's bright orange tiger paw logo.

The salvation of Jimmy Red may be tied to the bootleg whiskey trade. The 1840s blackface minstrelsy version of the folk song "Blue-Tail Fly" contains a lyric about Jim crack corn, which has been interpreted severally as a reference to rotgut liquor, livestock feed, and the milling process. This auburn-hued dent corn was supposedly favored by Black moonshiners, who hid their stills in woods and swamps behind their fields. This origin story about the makers of stump was subsequently seized by white millers who shouldn't profit from that narrative. The truth may be more straightforward. As Scott Blackwell of High Wire Distilling explained: "If you can get good grits out of a corn, you can make a good whiskey. There's a direct correlation between starch and sugar. And Jimmy Red's starch has character."

Amateur seedsman Ted Chewning, who farms in Colleton County, acquired three precious ears from a friend who died before harvesting his last crop, ensuring its tenuous existence. Chewning was able to trace the genesis to a farmer named Elmore Humphries, born in Screven, Georgia, about forty miles from the coast, in 1895. But that's where the trail stopped.

"I have some of [Chewning's] original Jimmy Red in the vaults across the street," Ward said. "This kernel is from the more purified line. It took ten years. We kept picking the best of the best plants in the field."

Roberts chimed in. "All maize was non-persistent, so without human intervention, it does not survive. That's fairly unique because most of the early staple cereals were self-pollinating and self-replicating. Corn is different: It doesn't replicate, it will cross, it'll drift, it does everything you don't want a plant to do. If you hit on something that tastes really good, you have to work hard to keep it the same."

We moved to a table where Ward had more antebellum corn varieties laid out. John Haulk, Bloody Butcher, White Eagle, Carolina Gourdseed White. Roberts ticked off kernel shapes: "There's every degree of cross from flint to dent here." To understand the evolution of grits in the South, he asserted, it's crucial to know the morphologies and classes of corn, because some are more suitable than others for fresh grits.

"If you've ever tried to hand quern flint corn? It's the hardest substance produced by the plant kingdom," he said. "And the reason you don't see grits in the North is because, as you move north, there's more and more flint class, and you can't make fresh grits from flint corn. Dent is much easier to mill. Even so, coarse grits originally came into fashion because nobody wanted to have to pass it through a hand mill again and again."

Roberts and I took a spin around the fields where grape, indigo, sorghum, and rice experiments were underway as Ward loaded his truck with bins of heritage field peas. CREC is based on a 325-acre farm that has been dedicated to agricultural research since the 1930s— after the Sea Island cotton industry collapsed, most planters shifted to vegetable "truck" farming; at its coastal facility, Clemson developed disease-resistant tomatoes, okra, beans, melons, and cabbage. Ward's rare seed studies reflected the rising interest in preserving the earlier Lowcountry pantry.

"Want to know a good definition of old-fashioned grits and why we miss them?" Roberts asked. "There used to be signs on the side of the best toll mills that would say 'fresh grits.' And that meant new crop, fully robust corn with bright field flavor, still carrying nuances of sweet corn, as well as minerality or dairy or nuts. To keep chunks of the germ, where the flavor resides, along with the hard-starch endosperm, you have to mill to a big particle size instead of milling it all to powder."

So why shift away from something that sounds so delicious?

"Instant grits were easy," Roberts said. "Coarse grits were the better way to get flavor out of a mill product but you give up speed. The cooking time is ninety minutes. Two hours are even better. Best? Soak it overnight, just let it ferment, expanding the flavor profile and nutrition of the corn. Then bring up the heat."

It was getting late, and hunger set in. Roberts walked me to my car. "Know what Native Americans call corn?" he asked.

I was stumped.

"Mother."

CORN SONG

The Catawba word for corn is kus.

"It was a really important crop for our people," Roo George-Warren said. An elected official of the Catawba Nation, one of his areas of expertise was food sovereignty. "To give you a sense of how central it was to our diet, when you say the word for bread, kustá, it has no etymological relationship to wheat. The closest thing to what Westerners would've called bread would be corn cakes." (Amelia Simmons included a recipe for "Indian Slapjack" in *American Cooking*, first published in 1796, prepared with what she called Indian meal.) And yet, the Catawba corn was lost. Or so they thought.

"We'd gone to all the growers in the tribe that we could find, and none of them had any of the seeds left over," said Aaron Baumgardner, a plant ecologist and tribal director of natural resources, when the three of us talked on a video call. "Through interviews with our elders, the thing that kept coming up over and over again was, 'We need to bring back the corn.'"

Yeh is-WAH h'reh, the People of the River, whose villages along the Catawba were established 6,000 years ago, finally found their corn, kus iswq, tucked in a seed repository at Davidson College in North Carolina. "It was labeled the 'Lial flint corn,'" Baumgardner said. "When it was brought into the extension office, the family said that they had gotten it from the Indians in the early 1800s." The Lials farmed in Hickory, and according to Baumgardner, the Catawbas were the only tribe in the area at the time. And the seed looked familiar. "It matched what we have in our archaeological sites. It also matched the visual descriptions that we find of the corn in our historical documents." He explained that the origin corn could be red, yellow, white or "rainbowy calico" in hue, and during the first year growing it again at the tribal farm in Rock Hill, South Carolina, they reclaimed five gallons of seed from the small jar given to George-Warren by the college. Bringing back the corn was not just an agricultural effort, because it was also so rooted in Catawba culture. "In addition to doing the seed saving, we're working to incorporate community into the corn again," George-Warren said, pointing to a corn husk doll on a bookshelf. "Because so much of our processes had ceremony around them. We can't lose these songs, and words, and dance, and recipes again."

The next step was to revive lost traditions for preparing the corn: nixtamalization in a pot of oak ash, then turning it into whole hominy or grinding it into meal.

"It's a bit smokier and has a really prevalent corn flavor, more so than Quaker grits would have," said George-Warren.

Baumgardner agreed. "I wasn't a fan until I had our grits."

George-Warren grinned. "And context for Aaron not liking grits? He grew up in Ohio."

The two of them told me they'd discovered another Catawba variety, a black sweet corn, most likely adopted after white settlers introduced a taste for it. Once grown by heritage seed keeper Carl "White Eagle" Barnes in Grove, Oklahoma, the seed was inherited by Braiding the Sacred, a network of Indigenous corn growers, who shared it back.

"We kind of have a new piece of history within our corn story," said George-Warren. "Traditions change, seeds exchange hands."

GRIST

When Pat Conroy published *The Prince of Tides* in 1986, my parents copied out full paragraphs and left them taped to the refrigerator for each other to find. Late at night, I could hear them snorting with laughter in our kitchen. Parts of chapter eleven were their absolute favorite, where Lila Wingo served sweetbreads and coq au vin to her shrimper husband in a quixotic attempt to be accepted in the Colleton League cookbook "containing the best recipes in the Lowcountry." As with the finest humor, it cut close to the bone.

My mother was a self-taught cook. The only two books in her pantry were *Larousse Gastronomique* and *Charleston Receipts*, which, like Conroy's fictional version, was compiled by ladies of a certain social standing. (My Nana's sister, Fannie Lee Anderson Seabrook, contributed a palmetto pickle recipe.) Mom's spoonbread was lighter than cotton candy, and her pan gravy smoother than velouté. She missed the soaking humidity of a Southern coastal summer, missed girlfriends who danced the shag on weekends at Myrtle Beach, missed other people who sounded like her. It was she who encouraged the social calls with family who remain rooted down there.

I would be less crazy if she hadn't.

To be of a place but not from it has been the crux of an unresolved identity crisis. Belonging to a Southern family eleven generations deep but living in a place where no one frankly gives a damn. Drifting into a softer accent, heavy on y'all, for every visit to the relatives still occupying those big white houses on Edisto and South of Broad. Would it help to fit in more if I liked that little white mound of food? Why do I want to fit in at all? I was born in Manhattan, for crying out loud.

The Lowcountry's most ballyhooed dish is shrimp and grits. Unlike other regions in the Grits Belt, where country ham or livermush or red-eye gravy is its companion on the plate, coastal South Carolina prefers shellfish for breakfast. The height of shrimping season and the corn harvest overlap—always on the horizon that time of year, the commercial boats, rigging extended, nets dragging, a-sway on the tidal swell. But the tiny sweet shrimp that swarm in salt marsh creeks, rippling across the water's surface like a gust of wind, are most prized for this dish. The best way to catch them is to wade in with a cast net, feet sinking in the plumey sediment of decaying bulrush and spartina grass.

The *Charleston Receipts* version called for fresh shrimp sauteed in bacon grease with an onion and bell pepper. Stock from the pinched heads, or shells and a little flour, was added until the whole mess was slightly soupy. A dash of cayenne, a slug of Worcestershire. Then poured over hot grits. Comfort food for homesick parents.

No one from Charleston used to order shrimp and grits in a sit-down restaurant. Coinciding with the revival of fresh grits milling, however, the dish has appeared on fancy menus for those who don't own a net or boat. I tried one version with cheese grits and a grossly sweet cube of cornbread on the side, and another drowning in mushroom gravy.

"You don't want it to look like prison food," one waiter said.

Or, I thought, albino puke from a cardboard cylinder.

According to a spokesperson at The Quaker Oats Company, the South continues to be the largest per capita consumer of instant grits, and perhaps nowhere was that more evident than in St. George, home to the World Grits Festival. Every April since 1986, this town in Dorchester County, 53 miles upcountry from Charleston, hosts a weekend celebration of grits eating and corn tossing. Almost 30,000 people attend. The festival highlight involves an inflatable kiddie pool brimming with viscous corn particles in a starch matrix. Contestants dive in, roll around, and then weigh themselves. The winner has the most grits adhered.

· · ·

Do not attempt this with Jimmy Red grits. While seed savers continue to propagate more heirlooms, ground corn of this kind has a rarified shelf life. Old kernels with a legendary past, surviving in an overlooked jar or cached in a porch fridge, are becoming rarer finds.

"On the cob, it's yellow," Ted Chewning said when he spoke to me on the phone from his farm in Walterboro. "And only turns blood red when it dries down. We're guessing it was a moonshine corn because of the way it finishes after fermenting. Throughout the history of whiskey in America, people saved their seeds. But it's still a mystery. We all love a mystery."

One morning, I cooked a pot of Johnsman's grits, flecked with telltale red bran. Low and slow for hours, in equal parts water and whole milk, it had chewy density. Some weird alchemy between this milled corn and dairy imparted creamy, cheesy goodness. The corn's flavor wasn't masked either. I ate a spoonful. Then another.

I didn't gag.

. . .

My mother missed the fresh grits renaissance. She died up North, unable to eat solid food, in the summer of 1989. Her ashes rode in the trunk when we drove her South for the last time. One Christmas before she got sick, however, my brother Jamie gave her a kitchen apron, silk-screened with the wisecrack made famous by her favorite *Alice* sitcom character Flo. It read: "Kiss My Grits."

She wore it with pride.

—Originally published June 2015

Author's Note: In the fall of 2020, Geechie Boy Mill changed its name to Marsh Hen Mill.

WHO OWNS UNCLE BEN?

"Don't stir the pot," Nana said.

Crowded together at the stovetop in her Queens Village apartment, my grandmother grabbed my hand away from the rice spoon. Her narrow kitchen contained an enamel sink, gas oven, and a Coldspot refrigerator stuffed with mystery scraps the elderly often can't bear to throw out, either a sign of lifelong frugality or early-stage dementia. Both possibilities wouldn't occur to me as a rude teenager who showed up occasionally to abuse her generosity—a quiet bedroom to myself, hot meals, season tickets to the opera—and in return would clean out the frost-crusted liver pudding, half-eaten bowls of grits, mold-crusted jars of pepper jelly. But I also never stayed long because, this being the late 1970s, our conversations were haunted by uncomfortable truths about our family history.

"Please don't bring your friends around."

I stared at her, confused. She sounded afraid.

"I mean those people who work with you."

Counselors at a summer camp for youth living in urban and underserved communities.

Her attitude held steadfast through the civil rights era: my grandmother was raised by parents who lived through the Civil War and passed their complicated causes to the next generation. After witnessing her battles with my slightly more progressive parents over racism, over religion, over politics, all over the turkey and greasy gravy at Thanksgiving gatherings, I had learned to simply let Nana show me how to cook rice properly.

She preferred Uncle Ben's Converted.

Yeah, I know.

LIKE WHITE ON RICE

My people were rice eaters. Marry into my family a potato or pasta eater, and we would convert you to brown rice, red rice, basmati and jasmine, Forbidden rice, arborio, and yes, even commercial brands of white rice.

But here's the issue. The roots of rice in the South troubled me. The story began when one branch of my father's family arrived in the late seventeenth century, Huguenot exiles from France, who first settled in Berkeley County, South Carolina. Within a generation they became wealthy planters. They mostly grew rice. They married Scottish merchants who sold rice. One of their grandsons would become a famous Revolutionary War hero, and in every passing generation someone got stuck with his name, all the way to my uncle Frank. My grandmother, Lydia Alta Anderson Mitchell, was born in 1893, one of eight daughters whose father was a storekeeper and circuit court judge. He managed to send them all to college in an era when many Southern women didn't have that opportunity. They were beautiful, funny, elitist, stubborn, both vengeful and loyal. Their collective nickname was the Queens of Edisto.

My grandfather, James Murray Mitchell, was Nana's sweetheart, a neighboring farmer's son with artistic aspirations, and by all accounts, a handsome rascal who talked her into leaving for New York during the 1920s. When he died suddenly, Nana was left alone to raise their three sons on a teacher's salary, and despite the urging of her family, never remarried or moved back home, but she always put food from home on the table: boiling hog heads in that apartment kitchen, diligently pouring bourbon on fruitcakes stored in a hallway closet, preserving pumpkins, Jerusalem artichokes, watermelon rinds, serving dishes based on rice raised with enslaved labor. Without her cooking, I would not have such a strong connection to my family's culinary legacy or the desire to rectify it. On multiple trips, I talked to others wrestling with the same issue, around the time when a white supremacist was on trial for murdering nine Black parishioners, and a Black Lives Matter activist was arrested for tackling a Secessionist Party protestor waving the Confederate battle flag.

. . .

Rice was fundamental to the Carolina Lowcountry kitchen, where the pot contained ingredients introduced from West African, Huguenot, and Caribbean Creole cultures, where Senegambian jollof became red rice and Parisian beignets de riz became calas and johnny cake. While imported grain established rice as a cash crop on the southern Atlantic coast by the late 1600s, a farmer named Hezekiah Mayham in 1786 planted the first documented field of the subtropical *japonica* that would eventually be called Carolina Gold.

The origin story of this "gold seed" is one of those quandaries still giving food historians and botanists heartburn. Scientists may be getting closer to cracking the genomic mystery, curiously enough, by tracing funeral practices involving rice that traveled from the Tana Taraja region in South Sulawesi to Madagascar. The name derives not only from the hue of the grain as it ripens, but also references the fortunes created as the demand grew for the starchy variety. Cookbooks, plantation diaries, and oral histories documented the profound influence of this crop. The wealthiest planters slept in Chippendale-style mahogany or cherry four-poster beds carved with panicles of rice. A long-handled silver spoon originally used in England for serving stuffing became a treasured heirloom on Charleston sideboards when placed next to bowls of rice. The spoons are still in demand. A cousin gave me one as a wedding gift.

The first mention of rice cookery in the South was an instruction on how "To Boil Rice," in Eliza Lucas Pinckney's personal 1770 receipt book. By 1847, when Sarah Rutledge published *The Carolina Housewife* at the height of antebellum rice culture, she included recipes for every meal, including rice crumpets, rice sponge cake, rice waffles, rice flummery, rice blancmange, rice milk. Her golden-crusted rice casseroles echo the masterpieces of Carême, in particular his Casserole au Riz à la Moderne; her pilau traces the journey of that most fragrant dish from the Persian Empire after the Arab conquest scattered the recipe to the four winds in the seventh century, and evolved into both paella and pullao, as well as arroz con pollo, jambalaya, and Hopping John. Even birds that feasted on Lowcountry rice became a prized dish—the bobolink is the New World epicurean equivalent of the ortolan. Its Latin name, *Dolichonyx oryzivorus*, refers to a voracious appetite for the grain, and it's still known regionally as the rice bird.

Rutledge did not cook for herself. She had kitchen help.

As more planters shifted to growing Carolina Gold, they paid a higher premium for enslaved people from the ancient rice regions of Sierra Leone and the Upper Guinea Coast; traders were quick to advertise these skills in auction posters at the Old Slave Mart on Chalmers Street in Charleston. Fields were dug by hand in the lowland meadows and cypress swamps surrounding the great tidal river deltas. Grain was sown by pressing it into the muddy ground with the bare heel, a technique first practiced in the freshwater floodplains of the Sahel of Africa. Harvest in the Lowcountry took place at the height of hurricane season. Panicles were cut and baled. Women pounded the hulls with a wooden mortar and pestle, and then winnowed while tossing handfuls from handwoven fanner baskets, husks blowing away in the wind. The grain was absurdly delicate and fractured easily during milling, producing "middlings" or "brokens" that became a delicacy of sorts as well. The entire process, from planting to polishing, was punishing work under a subtropical sun, with risk of exposure to malaria, cholera, and yellow fever. Malnutrition and mortality rates were high.

The enslaved grew their own rice as well.

Other varieties—particularly upland bearded rice introduced from Guinea—were planted in provision or kitchen gardens, plots granted by overseers to supplement meager rations of cornmeal and pork. The husk of this African rice was reddish-brown to purple in hue, and unlike the golden Asian variety, thrived in dry soil conditions rather than flooded fields. It arrived wherever Africans landed in the New World, including Trinidad, El Salvador, and French Guiana. The Maroons of Suriname still grow upland bearded rice, which plays a central role in their ancestor meals. The ceremony called ala mofo nyan, or food for all mouths, often includes offerings of African origin foods like pigeon peas and rice.

With the advent of Emancipation, commercial production of Carolina Gold gradually ceased. Berms, sluices, trunks, and dykes rotted and returned to swampland, the grain barges and settlement houses, abandoned, crumbled in decay, strangled by creeper vines. A series of devastating hurricanes between 1881 and 1911 wiped out the last vestiges of viable rice agriculture in the Lowcountry—the cost of revitalizing fields outweighed the potential profits. Carolina Gold barely escaped extinction as large-scale farming in Louisiana and Texas supplanted it. Upland bearded rice also disappeared as the rural population that once raised it left for northern industrial cities during the Great Migration. Certain stubborn seed savers planted these grains as a hobby, or to attract ducks during hunting season. Carolina Gold eventually had a comeback, but only as a specialty crop, not the goldmine of the antebellum era.

Why would anyone preserve a crop, no matter how flavorful and aromatic, with such a disturbing heritage?

BROKEN RICE

At Hannibal's Kitchen, Safiya Grant's rice was righteous.

Hannibal's had a narrow dining room with padded vinyl banquettes, a takeout counter, and a pass-through window offering a tantalizing view into a steamy kitchen. On a side street bounded by housing projects and industrial port facilities, in a squat cinder-block building painted haint blue, this Gullah restaurant resisted the gentrification swallowing gritty East Charleston block by block. It was slightly north of Emanuel African Methodist Episcopal Church, better known as Mother Emanuel to its parishioners, where Dylann Roof was welcomed to pray during Bible study on the evening of June 17, 2015. Like the church, Hannibal's Kitchen was a community pillar. A pillar built of collards, lima beans, turkey wings, and smoked neck bones, one of the few Black-owned restaurants south of the Neck. (Hannibal was the nickname of family patriarch Robert Lawrence Huger.) At the front door, a crowd waited for their orders. Waitresses dodged around with pitchers of sweet tea and platters of crab rice.

The crab rice here was a distant relative of ceebu jën, from the fishing communities on the island of Ndar, on the Senegal River. Drenched in butter and topped with shredded crabmeat and shrimp sautéed with bell pepper, celery, onion, and bacon, it referenced the mangrove swamps of West Africa as well as a Provençal pilau.

Blue crabs dwell in the creeks and salt marsh of the Lowcountry estuarine system. While only a few recipes were mentioned—deviled or stewed—in the earliest regional cookbooks, crab is foolishly easy to catch. An apocryphal tale has circulated in my family involving one of my great-uncles, a rope, and a dead dog, but usually a rank chicken neck gets their greedy attention. For several summers, when Nana brought me down on childhood visits to her sisters who still lived in Charleston, one of my happiest memories was the time spent barefoot and sunburnt on the end of a ramshackle dock jutting into the Folly River, net poised as crab after crab rose in the muddy brown water to my bait. The great-aunts got so fed up picking crab day after day that they slipped the full bucket out of the kitchen and dumped them back into the marsh to crawl away again. Nana never mixed crab with rice. Shrimp, yes. Crab, no. Not sure why, but it may have something to do with that dog. So, I was grateful for the introduction to this version at Hannibal's Kitchen.

Safiya Grant had a long, thin face framed by gold earrings. She slid into a booth opposite me, and her daughter, dressed for a dance class, climbed into her lap.

"You want a little something-something with that? Get the red rice and collards, too."

Another platter arrived. Her red rice was the real deal, the consequence of tomatoes and chili peppers introduced to Africa, and returned, transformed, on the Middle Passage.

Grant tilted her head in concentration when I asked how she cooked it.

"First, you fry the meat," she said. "And you can use any flavor of meat, that's the flavor your red rice is going to be. Italian sausage, beef sausage. Then, you add some veggies, onions, and bell peppers, and put the sauce in, whatever seasoning, and water, stir it up to make it smooth, some salt and pepper, and whatever rice you want. It's an equal share, one to one, cook it until halfway, and for your eye, if you want it a little redder, add some more sauce."

"What kind of rice?" I asked.

"Any kind. It doesn't matter."

Before Grant's family bought the business, two other owners operated restaurants at the same address. The Hugers eventually changed the menu—she was the third generation to cook there.

"In the '60s, they used to have bologna sandwiches, cornbread, that kind of thing," Grant said. "People who went to school around here, they used to jump the fence—hope you don't get caught—it was like a snack place for them. Teachers would send across to get lunch and stuff, too."

Grant's daughter squirmed out of her lap and danced away. I scraped the rest of my lunch into a clamshell. Before she disappeared back into the clatter of the kitchen, I asked Grant a parting question.

"Where do you get your rice?"

She smiled.

"Bulk, from Costco."

GRAINS OF WISDOM

Not long after rice production failed in the Lowcountry, German scientist Erich Gustav Huzenlaub and British chemist Francis Heron Rogers invented a method of parboiling commercially produced rice to retain greater nutritional value. The Huzenlaub Process yielded a less starchy grain resistant to weevils. It was also the color of a manila folder. The original patent number 368,092 application filed in Great Britain on November 30, 1939, claimed: "The method of this invention produces the highest degree of gelatinization possible in a rice grain, leaving it totally free from any white, chalky, light refracting spots or sections on the grain surface or grain interior, it produces a rice grain without any hint of colouration beyond the slightly creamy tint that which is usually regarded as a characteristic of the very highest grades of rice, and it produces further a rice grain which is free from any objectionable odor during subsequent cooking."

Objectionable odor?

American businessman and candy heir Forrest E. Mars Sr. acquired a stake in the patent for this easy-to-cook "converted" rice in 1942. The first Converted Rice Inc. plant set up in Houston subjected Gulf Coast grain to Huzenlaub's parboiling; the company then obtained a wartime government contract to supply rice to US Army mess kitchens on fighting fronts from Europe to Africa. By 1947, when it arrived in American grocery stores, the brand acquired a name and a face on the packaging: a genial elder servant wearing a waiter's jacket and bowtie, with an honorific historically reserved by white Southerners who avoided calling Black men "Mister."

Uncle Ben may never have existed, although Mars Inc. corporate lore referenced a Black rice farmer, last name unknown, in Beaumont, Texas, as his inspiration. A waiter named Frank Brown, however, who worked at the Tavern Club in Chicago, did consent to have his portrait painted for $500. The restaurant was a favorite haunt for the agency reps who created the first advertising campaign featuring his image, which appeared in *Life Magazine* on October 27, 1947. Tag line? "The sunny-colored rice that cooks white." In six years, the brand became the top-selling packaged long-grain rice in the country.

· · ·

A curious thing happened in 1971. Uncle Ben disappeared from the packaging. This was the tumultuous year when President Richard M. Nixon made disparaging remarks about women, Blacks, Mexicans, and Italians on secret White House tapes. The Supreme Court overturned the draft-evasion conviction of Muhammad Ali and, in *Swann v. Charlotte-Mecklenburg Board of Education*, also upheld the use of busing to achieve racial desegregation in schools. Three drunken white males in Drew, Mississippi, killed Jo Etha Collier, an 18-year-old Black woman. James Earl Ray, Martin Luther King Jr.'s assassin, was caught in a jailbreak attempt in Tennessee. The Black Panthers were accused of an attack at the Ingleside police station in San Francisco that left one officer dead. Don Cornelius debuted as the host of *Soul Train*.

Uncle Ben returned to the box in 1983.

Nana died the next year.

"Help yourself."

Not only was this her invocation at the table, the invitation to an open refrigerator, and even the welcome to a stash of bourbon in her liquor cabinet, but also a battle cry for an independent woman who lived ninety-two years, never said a peep about money missing from her purse or unwritten thank-you notes, and cried down the phone line when her uppity granddaughter got a scholarship to Vassar. Until the end, she also never burned a pot of rice on that modest stove so far from the salt marsh.

Two decades later, in 2007, Mars Inc. hired another agency to promote Uncle Ben to chairman of the board. He was reimagined in a lavish corner office, in a bright blue suit, still wearing the same bowtie, and dispensing "grains of wisdom." Socially-minded critics were ambivalent about the campaign's intent.

. . .

The series titled *Unenslaved: Rice Culture Paintings* by Gullah artist Jonathan Green was kaleidoscope bright and full of movement. Men pole barges loaded impossibly high with grain. A woman in a polka dot dress and headscarf tossed rice with a fanner basket. Others toted sheaves in fields stretching to a low marshy horizon. For its debut with the Gibbes Museum of Art in Charleston, in 2014, the series was paired with the earlier work of white watercolorist Alice Ravenel Huger Smith, who depicted life on an antebellum rice plantation in softer hues. Her work was now considered racially fraught.

"I wanted to capture it from the perspective of Africans in touch with their own humanity and dignity," Green said, who showed me a painting from the series when we met in his Charleston studio. "I wanted to think of the history of the Lowcountry and rice as I know it from *my* ancestors."

The soft-spoken artist was born in Gardens Corner, not far from the island where Nana grew up.

"I love the fact that you can have two impressions of the same culture," Green said. "How we do not know each other, even though we've been living side by side for hundreds of years? How is it that we have allowed ourselves to treat each other like this for so long? Painting this series as if Africans came here like everyone else, that helped me overcome this fog of slavery."

"What rice did you eat growing up?" I asked.

"My grandmother cooked Carolina Gold. She grew it. But my mother didn't go out into the rice field," he said. "She used Uncle Ben's or Mahatma. I cook the way my grandmother did. She put some oil in the pan and then the rice. Threw vegetables in there with the rice, peas, or whatever, and when the vegetables were cooked and the rice brown enough, she added the liquid."

The Requiem for Rice was Green's next project. The multimedia collaboration with filmmaker Julie Dash and composer Trevor Weston was "a lamentation for repose of the souls of the dead who were enslaved, exploited, and brutalized on Lowcountry South Carolina and Georgia's rice plantations and who remain unburied, unmourned, and unmarked." It premiered at Charleston's Color of Music Festival in 2017. Green commissioned scholar Edda Fields-Black, who taught the transnational history of Gullah Geechee culture at Carnegie Mellon University, to write the libretto. She was an expert on rice agriculture in West Africa.

Dr. Fields-Black told me: "Never met a rice field that I didn't love, and literally would have to pull on my boots and want to get into."

She also spent childhood trips visiting her Lowcountry family; her father's ancestors are buried on several plantations that once belonged to Nathaniel Heyward, whose vast estate included 1,648 enslaved at the time of his death. For her libretto, she drew on the journals of abolitionist Fanny Kemble and oral histories from the Depression-era Works Progress Administration Slave Narrative Project.

"I want to bring these experiences to light and create something beautiful about a labor system that was pretty horrible," Fields-Black said. "We're using the metaphor of a mass said for the dead, but it's very much our own creation, an African American requiem."

When I talked to her on the phone in Pittsburgh, she admitted never eating rice as a child. "White bread, white potatoes, white rice. My father associated these with poverty and obesity. Now, if I don't eat rice—brown rice—every day, I get cranky."

GHOST RICE

Lucie Kulze climbed on the vintage Allis-Chalmers combine when it stalled. She peered into the unloader as her uncle and father fixed the belt drive. The autumn sky was streaked with cloud, insects hummed in the heat, and a breeze rattled the palmettos. Grain hung heavy, all green and golden. Everyone wore snake boots and kept an eye on the riverbank when a bull alligator coughed. White egrets startled as the combine lurched back into motion, rattling away and burping out chaff, chomping through a rice field bounded by centuries-old canals. Despite the calm day, Hurricane Matthew was barreling toward the Carolina coast. Farmers scrambled.

Kulze was a cousin, our blood tied by multiple generations and entwined family trees. Nana and her great-grandmother were sisters. The 22-year-old brunette had ramrod posture, preferred secondhand work clothes from the Salvation Army store, and instead of pursuing mainstream higher education, chose apprenticeships ranging from permaculture to animal husbandry. One of her mentors was Dr. Brian Ward. When her family got a grant to restore the ruined dykes and trunks on their Combahee River property, they started growing Charleston Gold.

This was rice I might learn to respect.

In 1998, two rice scientists collaborated on a new grain by crossbreeding Carolina Gold with sturdier *japonica* varieties. After ten years of testing and selection, Gurdev Khush and Merle Shepard brought the grain to Anna McClung, a geneticist at the USDA Agricultural Research Service in Beaumont, Texas. (Remember Beaumont? Where a Black rice farmer named Ben reportedly toiled?)

Dr. Shepard told me: "One of the parents of Charleston Gold is a modern, high-yielding 'green revolution' rice, but I asked Dr. Khush to keep the gold color on the hull and add an aromatic gene from a basmati. Dr. McClung did the final 'cleaning up' of the variety and grew it in regional trials." Of the eleven historic rice rivers in South Carolina, the Combahee is the tenth in succession from north to south, where Alice Smith painted her plantation scenes and several present-day landowners, including my cousins, were growing these new grains.

The Allis-Chalmers made several more passes through patches of rice ready to harvest, filling two large totes with 700 pounds of grain, which Kulze hauled by tractor back to her parents' house. She transferred the raw rice to smaller plastic bins and bags, setting up electric fans in the kitchen to aid the drying process. The room smelled of grass. A pot of rice simmered on the stove for dinner.

"What is ghost rice?" I asked.

"That's when the plant makes a panicle, and the hull is there, but with no grain inside," Kulze said. "Like it didn't fill. Dr. Ward says it happens when the soil is high in organic matter."

• • •

Before driving down from Charleston for the harvest, I stopped at the farmers market in Marion Square, and bought bags of freshly picked field peas. If I had an ancestor meal, food for all mouths, it would be Hopping John. Nana said my grandfather ate his cowpeas and rice topped with a big glob of mayonnaise. My father preferred it that way as well. Yes, sounds gross, but it's obviously a white people thing. Always cowpeas, never black-eyed peas. Everyone had opinions about the potlikker and whether the flavor meat should be bacon or a smoked ham hock. No one could agree about the name either. Some argue Hopping John, or Hoppin' John for the colloquially precious, was a bastardization of pois de pigeon. Others swear a lame pea vendor named John once limped through the streets of Charleston. Sarah Rutledge recommended garnishing the dish with a sprig of mint, so don't give me grief about mayonnaise. In *The Savannah Cookbook* (1933), Harriet Ross Colquitt wrote: "As children, it was our custom, when the word went around that we were to have Hopping John for dinner, to gather in the dining-room, and as the dish was brought on to hop around the table before sitting down to the feast." Her recipe collection was illustrated with cartoonish images of possum hunts and vegetable sellers, and headnotes peppered with disparaging remarks about "coloreds" and "dark horses," ugly names close to those Nana used as well.

Dinner with Lucie Kulze was plain and simple. Rice with peas, the last bolted greens from the vegetable garden, some leftover succotash, and venison shot in the piney woods that backed up against the golden fields where, in two days' time, the remaining crop would be obliterated by hurricane-force winds and rain. The Charleston Gold was aromatic and fluffy, not split or starchy, complaints I often had against rice lacking conversion.

"What do you think about the history of rice here?" I asked.

"Truth is truth," she said. "When I'm out there working, I can't understand how it used to be done by hand, turning those swamps into fields. It's almost like Machu Picchu, but in a more buggy, snakey, alligatory environment. Tough as hell."

Kulze spared me two pounds of Charleston Gold to take home. I hugged this young girl who wore scruffy overalls and ate table scraps cold out of the fridge because she can't stand to see them go to waste.

At first light, she dragged the salvaged rice out into the last sun prior to the storm, in hopes of dehydrating the grain more before shipping it to a mill in Orangeburg. As I left her to it, she said: "Every single step has been a mountain and this year has more mountains than last."

Pot, stirred.

—Originally published June 2017

Author's Note: In 2020, Mars Inc. changed the name of its rice brand to Ben's Original, and dropped the image of a Black servant from packaging. Dr. Fields-Black published Combee, *an account of Harriet Tubman and her pivotal role in leading the Combahee River Raid of 1863 to liberate hundreds of enslaved people.*

HOT WET GOOBERS

"Stop the car," I shouted. "Pull over now. Now!"

We were driving on a county road near the Georgia border. My husband, Bronson, startled, swerved to the shoulder, and I flung open the passenger door to run back to a makeshift stand—two sawhorses, a plank, and a pot—tended by an old man sitting in a lawn chair under a live oak.

Returning to the car, I offered the soggy paper sack.

"What. . . ?"

"Just try them," I said. "Stick one in your mouth."

"They look disgusting. Don't let that drip on the mat."

Bronson was from New Jersey. I watched him cautiously shell and eat his first boiled peanut.

"Oh, my God."

"See?"

That was years ago. And we're still married.

THE PEANUT BELT

The peanut belongs to the New World, but it's a long journey from genesis to a boiled peanut stand in Georgia. Somewhere in the Bolivian Andes, two wild plant ancestors cross-pollinated 10,000 years ago to create the hybrid *Arachis hypogaea*, a scientific reference to how this weedy member of the legume family grows under the earth. From its center of origin, cultivation spread into Brazil, Argentina, Peru, Mexico, and the Caribbean; when the Portuguese and Spanish arrived, colonizers added it to their pantries as well. In 1570, explorer and naturalist Gabriel Soares de Souza noted cooks in Bahia had begun to exchange peanuts for Old World nuts in recipes "cut and covered with a sugar mixture as confections . . . candied and cured in long thin pieces." Portuguese traders introduced the peanut to their colony in China, now the world's biggest producer, and also ports in West Africa, where indigenous cousins, especially the Bambara groundnut, or *Vigna subterraneana*, were already a subsistence crop.

It also became a provision on slave ships. Known to Kongo speakers as *nguba* or *mpinda*, these root words evolved into "goober" and "pindar" when enslaved African Americans subsequently planted them in their kitchen allotments. In *Notes on the State of Virginia*, Thomas Jefferson documented the cultivation of peanuts there by 1781—he planted sixty-five hills of "peendars" and remarked during his presidency they were very sweet. Henry Wansey, a member of the Bath and West of England Agricultural Society, ate roasted nuts on his tour of America in 1794. He is credited with the first located use of the word "pea-nut." During the Denmark Vesey Conspiracy of 1822 in Charleston, a conjurer named Gullah Jack was reported to instruct plotters to eat parched corn and groundnuts, and carry a crab claw in their mouths as an amulet for invulnerability. Confederate troops ate them as an emergency ration. Consequently, the goober pea song. The sheet music first printed by a Confederate sympathizer is jokingly credited to A. Pindar (words) and P. Nutt (music). The sort of tune that could become an earworm:

"Sitting by the roadside on a summer's day, chatting with my mess-mates passing time away. Lying in the shadows, underneath the trees. Goodness, how delicious, eating goober peas. Peas, peas, peas, peas. Eating goober peas."

Peanuts have become an aspect of our intangible cultural heritage, essential to tailgate parties, baseball games, political rallies, school lunches, state fairs, circuses, and even prison commissaries. Roasted, parched, buttered, and raw. Southerners truly love them boiled. Slippery on the outside, chewy in the pod. Those who slurp oysters raw but think "country caviar" tastes like snot? Shame on you. My father loved eating them with a Grape Nehi, but I preferred an ice-cold Coke, with enough throat-choking fizz to kill down the salt. Unlike my husband, I don't recall eating my first boiled peanut but haven't forgotten the outrage when vendors first introduced new flavorings to the brine. Cajun spice? Old Bay? BBQ rub? Boiled peanuts always seemed within reach during my childhood summers, at the height of the harvest, when stands spontaneously popped up on the two-lane highways of the Peanut Belt.

"It's serendipitous," said Matt Lee, who co-authored *The Lee Bros. Boiled Peanuts Catalogue* with his brother Ted. "Never know when you'll come across a good one."

BIG PEANUT

Alex Hardy remembered his grandfather plowing fields with a mule. A rawboned man in his late 60s, he surveyed row after row of peanut vines as a harvester churned past, uprooting the late season crop with a little shimmy to shake off the sandy Georgia soil. A tractor followed, pulling a combine that threshed the nuts and spewed out chaff. The swirling dust was ballet-slipper pink. Hardy's wife, Jacque, a retired studio photographer, picked up a handful of green nuts left on the ground and cracked them open.

"At one time, Alex's granddaddy had a stable of thirty-eight mules," she said.

"They were a prized possession," he said, nodding. "Couldn't do without them. My daddy had a mule for a year or two but quickly switched to tractors once he got out the war."

Hardy's family migrated to Pulaski County, Georgia, in the late eighteenth century, and for generations farmed at the tail end of the Atlantic Coastal Fall Line, the geologic boundary where the outwash plain of the upper continental shelf deposited sandy, loamy soil, which happened to be paradise for raising peanuts, give or take a bankrupting drought. The lesser roads in this part of the state were lined with pecan groves and loblolly pine. Before forced onto the Trail of Tears, the Creek Confederacy had its capital here; Sherman's March to the Sea passed to the north. And the extended Hardy family currently owned one of the larger peanut operations in south Georgia, which included an oil-roasting plant and a packing warehouse. They also farmed 1,000 acres of peanuts. More than half were green nuts selected for boiling.

"Our first year, we planted three acres," Hardy said. "That yielded 10,000 pounds. Sold them in gallon buckets and trash bags. Now we're up to a million pounds."

. . .

We climbed back into Hardy's pickup and drove to the warehouse, a red-trimmed, metal-sided facility on US Highway 341, close by the family farmhouse and an artificial lake where the grandchildren fished until an alligator interloped. Nuts from the field wagons were being loaded into bulk containers, then passed through a cleaning system and tumbled along conveyor belts as contract workers processed them, picking out stray stems and imperfect pods. Seasonal workers were bused in daily from Americus, an hour and a half away. The break room had signs in English and Spanish. Forklifts moved pallets of bushel bags into cold storage. Most of the green harvest would be shipped to supermarket chains like Kroger and Winn-Dixie, or picked up by wholesale distributors with customers farther north.

"We send one or two semi loads a day to New York, and it all winds up in Chinatown," Hardy said. "Chinese, Africans, Indians. They might not cook them the way we do, but it's a good market. A guy originally from Gambia buys them for Minnesota. We also pack out a one-ounce size; you know, the kind on airplanes, for colleges and farm organizations. And a two-ounce size, believe it or not, for the prison system."

. . .

Peanuts are a singularly Southern crop because they need 140 frost-free days to mature. They were historically grown in fields from Virginia to Texas, and more recently expanded into Arkansas and southern Missouri. Seedsman John Coykendall was even spreading the gospel of Bambara groundnuts in Tennessee. But Georgia remained the epicenter of peanut farming.

Hardy explained that the four commercial varieties were Spanish, Valencia, Runner, and Virginia. He grew Jumbo Georgia Runners. "We've got twenty-five roadside stands and sell the Runners there. They are the preferred flavor for the connoisseurs and those who have the palate and know the difference. We've tried the Virginias, but customers will turn around and walk off."

We passed through plastic curtains into the boiling room, where his nephew Ken Hardy supervised the steam kettles. Measuring bowls brimmed with spice mix. Brining salt was piled against the wall. Ken boiled them at home, too. Adding ham hocks to the brine for flavor was his next day-off project.

"A peanut will not take in the salt until the heat's turned off," he said. "I've wanted to try this with ham hocks at home, but I need pantyhose to put them in, and my wife won't give me a pair."

His uncle smiled.

"In 1991, we decided to add on value to the crops we were growing," Hardy said. "We couldn't get boiled peanuts the way we liked them, fresh out of the field. The green peanut is bright and pretty and has sweetness to it. They're harvested before full maturity and still at the tender stage."

"When do you eat boiled peanuts, and what do you drink with them?" I asked.

"Usually watching the game," he said. "Best to me? Beer. Otherwise, Coke."

. . .

Since I was driving deeper into Georgia that night, we went into nearby Hawkinsville for lunch at a cafeteria opposite the train tracks. The Hardys greeted neighbors at other tables, and then heaped their plates with fried chicken, stewed tomatoes, and collards from the buffet. Dessert was yellow sheet cake with peanut butter caramel icing. A waitress brought over a pitcher of sweet tea. Hardy removed his AgGeorgia Farm Credit gimme cap and placed a paper napkin on his lap.

"Peanuts, to me, that's the perfect food," he said. "They say with water and a piece of bread and peanut butter you can live."

Jacque refilled my tea glass.

"Like every Southern town, you never go to the ball game of any sort that you don't see peanut hulls everywhere," she said. "And yesterday, in the next county, we went down there with a little wagon and gave away peanuts at a fundraiser boil for Lieutenant Governor Casey Cagle."

Hardy walked over to the cash register to pay for lunch. I asked how he felt about the season ending.

"More glad than sad. I'm ready for a break. It's so demanding."

Jacque chimed in.

"We have a little boy at church, he's probably five, you never see him but he says, 'When are the peanuts going to be gone? I hate to see them leave. Tell me they're going to be around for a bit longer.'"

We headed back to their farmhouse. Jacque tapped me on the shoulder and pointed out the truck window to an unexceptional meadow surrounded by oaks.

"As we're passing, see that monument in the yard? Confederate president Jefferson Davis camped right there the night before he was captured by Northern soldiers."

WILL WORK FOR PEANUTS

Remember when Jimmy Carter had to sell his peanut farm?

Actually, the Carter family still owns it.

Plains was even smaller than Hawkinsville, with a population of 573, including the two who required a permanent Secret Service detail posted outside their white clapboard house. On the outskirts of town, a grain silo complex, cotton warehouse, and transfer station for peanut wagons were clustered. Main Street consisted of two commercial blocks and was bisected by a rail line, which passed next to the whistle-stop depot that served as the thirty-ninth president's campaign headquarters.

Every September, Plains celebrated the peanut harvest with parade floats and a road race. A peanut princess was crowned. Concession stands sold funnel cakes and shaved ice. The Carters signed books at the antique store. In the account of his childhood, *An Hour Before Daylight*, he wrote:

"I began selling boiled peanuts on the streets of Plains when I was five years old. This was my first acquaintance with the outside world. As soon as the nuts began to mature on the vines, I would take my little wagon into one of the fields nearest our house, pull a load of peanut vines out of the ground, carry them home, pick the peanuts off the vines, wash them, and soak them in salty water overnight. The next morning, as early as possible, I boiled the peanuts for a half-hour or so until they were cooked but still firm, filled about twenty half-pound paper sacks (forty on Saturdays), and carried them to town in a basket, either walking down the railroad tracks or riding on my bike."

. . .

By the time I arrived, one morning after eating green nuts in the Hardys' fields, the parade was over and the Nobel Prize laureate away from home. I bought a bag of boiled Georgia Runners and a used copy of *The Carter Family Favorites Cookbook* (1977) in a gift shop. A chapter was devoted to peanut recipes: peanut butter brownies, peanut praline cakes, bacon and peanut butter cornbread, peanut vegetable loaf, peanut butter fondue. The high school Jimmy Carter and his wife Rosalynn attended had been converted to a museum and contained memorabilia from their childhood and political campaigns. The grinning peanut logo—based on Carter's own generous smile—was singularly weird. On display in a hall were peanut drawings by schoolchildren who have visited the National Historic Site.

More compelling was the Jimmy Carter Boyhood Farm, a few miles outside of town in the rural community of Archery, named for a nineteenth-century relief organization of the African Methodist Episcopal Church. Originally the modest house lacked running water and electricity, and the family cook prepared meals on a wood-fired stove. The dining room table was set with plastic replicas of fried chicken, deviled eggs, iced tea—a homespun reminder of how the Carters would eventually entertain in a bigger white house. The garden supplied the family with vegetables, and a dry goods store on the property operated by Carter's father supplied the neighbors, predominantly Black farmers and railroad employees. Walking around the quiet yard gave me a better sense of how growing up on the farm shaped the president's commitment to service, starting with early morning chores and his first commercial venture as a boiled-peanut vendor.

While Carter served in the Oval Office, he placed the family businesses into a blind trust to avoid conflict of interest. An Atlanta lawyer named Charles Kirbo was appointed financial trustee. Suffice to say, he did not do well by Jimmy Carter. After three years of drought and mismanagement, the plain-speaking president left the White House and discovered he was over $1 million in debt and dangerously close to losing the family farm.

Carter saved the fields with a book deal and the sale of his family's processing plant. His life in public service extended long beyond his term as president, most notably with the founding of the Carter Center, whose peace and health initiatives extended around the world. Even in his early 90s, he continued to volunteer with Habitat for Humanity, which had its headquarters in nearby Americus. But in 2013, the former leader of the free world admitted: "I'm a peanut farmer at heart, still grow peanuts on my farm in Georgia."

TOUGH NUTS

The Reverend Wayland Fuller Dunaway recorded a rare stanza of the "Goober Peas" song when confined at the Union prison on Johnson's Island, Ohio, during the latter half of the Civil War. Dunaway was serving as a captain in Company I of the 40th Virginia Infantry when captured during the Battle of Falling Waters in July 1863. In the opposing army, W. H. Shelton, an officer with the First New York Artillery, was incarcerated in 1864 but escaped from a Confederate prison camp in Columbia, South Carolina; as he fled toward Union lines, emancipated Blacks offered him goobers to eat. Shelton noted he was regularly provided "boiled peanuts, which was a favorite way of cooking when the bean was too green to bake." And in March of 1865, two months from surrender, General Robert E. Lee was quoted as saying to his son, G. W. Custis Lee: "I have been up to see the Congress and they do not seem to be able to do anything except to eat peanuts and chew tobacco, while my army is starving."

Peanuts kept showing up in dire circumstances, whether on slave ships or war zones, because they were packed with protein and insanely nourishing. Bob Parker, president of the National Peanut Board, told me: "It's the No. 1 food requested by food banks. When there is a natural disaster, we send peanut butter to those areas." Parker cited Project Peanut Butter, of St. Louis, which produced and distributed RUTF (ready-to-use therapeutic food) peanut paste to combat child malnutrition in Ghana, Malawi, Sierra Leone, and elsewhere. He also referenced MANA, another peanut paste produced in Georgia, distributed by UNICEF and other aid organizations.

"A one-ounce bag of peanuts will carry you a long time," he said. "And peanut butter is in 94 percent of American pantries."

. . .

George Washington Carver did not invent peanut butter. That's one of those conflated facts taught in grade school, much like everyone still believing the earth was flat in the fifteenth century when Columbus discovered America. Actual first honors go to a Canadian, Marcellus Gilmore Edson, who was issued US Patent No. 306727 for his "flavoring paste" to be used in the manufacture of "peanut-candy" on October 21, 1894. (Pre-Columbian Aztecs also pounded peanuts into a paste, so nothing is really new in the New World.) But Carver's botanical research at the Tuskegee Institute contributed greatly to peanut butter's rise in popularity. In 1916, he published a bulletin titled "How to Grow the Peanut & 105 Ways of Preparing It for Human Consumption," with his recipes for soup, cookies, fudge, and mock chicken. He also recommended peanuts for making shampoo, mayonnaise, paint, massage oil, and flour. The Carvoline cosmetics company of Birmingham, Alabama, manufactured peanut hair pomade with his endorsement.

It is unlikely Carver would have imagined the use devised by twelve inmates at Walker County Jail in Jasper, Alabama, on a Sunday evening in July 2017. They saved peanut butter from their sandwiches and molded it like clay to alter a number above a door leading outside, then tricked a rookie guard into opening it. (The employee thought he was letting them back into the cells.) The prisoners ditched their orange jumpsuits, flung blankets over the razor wire fence, and busted out. Most didn't get far—two were captured at the Flying J truck stop in town. At a news conference the next day, county sheriff James E. Underwood said: "Changing some numbers on the door with peanut butter—that may sound crazy, but these people are crazy like a fox."

When I reached Jasper Mayor Paul Liollio for comment, he wrote back: "This wasn't Jasper's finest hour."

LITTLE PEANUT

Nat Bradford tipped a pail of Carolina African Runners into the blast path of an industrial fan, scattering chaff and dust and twigs on his driveway. His farm also sat near the Fall Line, in Sumter, South Carolina, about 275 miles northeast from the Hardys' spread in Hawkinsville. Here the loamy soil was military tan, the fields of soy and cotton fronted by evangelical churches, and small white crosses marking traffic accidents sprouted next to kudzu-smothered fire hydrants. Thunderclouds were stacked in the distance, promising relief from the scorching upcountry heat, but the swarming gnats were relentless whenever Bradford shut off the fan to inspect the odd little nuts piling up in a plastic tub.

"It's an old, persnickety heirloom," he said, adjusting his Clemson visor. An eighth-generation farmer, the 43-year-old landscape architect specialized in growing persnickety crops on ten acres. He battled drought stress, late spring frosts, thrips, weed competition, and tomato spotted virus to grow this bijou peanut organically. (It's one-quarter the size of a Virginia Jumbo.) Now he was experimenting with threshing and winnowing techniques to prevent losing a huge percentage of his yield.

"The last time this nut was harvested? It was done by hand in the 1920s. It's not suited to modern-day, mechanized farming," he said, waving toward the scant bag at his feet. "But I'd rather have all my peanuts here than scattered on the field. Last year I was out there with a rake and a leaf blower, figuring out how to get them. And when you turn those peanuts over and the deer find them, they'll put a hurt on them, so you don't want them to sit long."

Bradford was one of the seed savers working to revive *Arachis hypogea var. Carolina African*. This foundational variety was thought to have arrived by slave ship at the end of the seventeenth century, and raised by enslaved people in the West Indies and the Southeast, essentially returning full circle a landrace crop to native soil.

These were likely the goober peas of song and story.

. . .

One of my favorite narratives about the Carolina African Runner involved the maumas of Charleston, elderly women who peddled a peanut-and-molasses candy known as groundnut cake. Sold for a penny, it was a humble treat that transitioned from the street to grander kitchens on the peninsula. Sarah Rutledge listed two recipes in *The Carolina Housewife*, one of which had a close resemblance to the candy observed by Soares de Souza in colonial Brazil more than two centuries earlier. In her influential Reconstruction-era recipe collection, *Mrs. Hill's New Cook Book* (1872), Annabella P. Hill, who lived through the Civil War in LaGrange, Georgia, not too far north of Plains, had a recipe for ground pea candy that resembled taffy, with additions of coconut and almonds. Earlier versions included egg whites, brandy, and lemon peel.

Few in living memory recalled what groundnut cake tasted like, as Charleston street vendors were put out of business by a sanitation ordinance before the Depression, and the Carolina African Runner nearly vanished as larger peanuts prevailed. A remaining handful of stock sat dormant in a seed bank at North Carolina State University. The persistence of horticultural preservationists gave it a comeback chance. Reviving groundnut cake was the parallel task of culinary historians like Gullah chef Benjamin "BJ" Dennis, who sat with me at a picnic table outside Rodney Scott's Whole Hog BBQ in Charleston before I drove upcountry to Sumter.

"We've still got the same palate as our ancestors," he said. "True Gullah Geechee food is really more related to what you see in West Africa. Those candies were molasses-based, that was the dominant sweetener, fresh ground from the sugar cane. But it can overwhelm. You want to taste that peanut. Those are the characteristics we're still trying to re-create."

His research took him to the southernmost Caribbean.

"The story got deeper when I went to Trinidad, and saw toolum, monkey meat, and groundnut cake candies being sold there," he said. "It was interesting talking to people in the West Indies and looking back at desserts from West Africa. It seemed like a typical dessert of the diaspora."

"How do you eat boiled peanuts?" I asked.

"I treat my peanuts like a bean, not cooked to mush, gotta have a little bite, salt, and chili flake. If I dump them over the sink into a strainer, I don't usually leave the sink. They don't last long."

. . .

When Bradford finished winnowing, the two of us went back out in the field. We stopped at a drying shed where several wagons parked. He had me climb up the side and stick my nose in the one containing his Carolina African Runners. The aroma nearly knocked me to the ground. It smelled like childhood.

"It's the tastiest peanut I've eaten," Bradford said.

"This is your whole crop?"

"We may get 3,200 pounds if everything is firing on all cylinders, but we're already a foot in the hole because plants don't even want to look at processing less than several eighteen-wheelers at a time. Might take a while to crack that nut."

Bradford scooped out several more bushel bags.

"If we can scale it up, I think this nut has a really good chance of getting out of the niche market. That's my dream, to have a wagon full one day. Not the bottom of a wagon."

"What's your favorite way to eat peanuts?"

"Boiled. If you can harvest them young, they are juicy and the shells are so thin you can eat the whole peanut. I like mine to be a little spicy, Cajun style. And I'm definitely a beer person. Really start to hanker for those dark beers, porters and stouts, this time of year. Oh, my word."

Bradford's oldest son needed a ride to a football game, an hour away, and I was mindful of driving back to Charleston with late-season thunderheads in my way. He gave me a bag of nuts to carry away.

"How many kids?" I asked.

"Got five," he said. "That's four generations in a row with four boys and a girl. Think maybe it's terroir. If it has an effect on food and plants, why wouldn't it have an effect on us?"

NUTS TO YOU

"Could you please stop making a big mess?"

My husband surveyed our kitchen with dismay. A dozen cookbooks lay open, peanut shells scattered, a precious cup of Carolina African Runners parched in a cast iron skillet. The groundnut candy recipe in *The Carolina Housewife* required boiling the mixture over a slow fire. How to interpret that? And the parched nuts: skins on or off? Mindful of the conversation with Benjamin Dennis, I substituted

Sapelo Purple Ribbon cane syrup for harsher molasses. Dennis was right to want this precious nut dominant.

"Want to try one?" I asked, offering a plate of the cooled candies.

"I don't want to loosen my fillings," Bronson said.

"Oh, come on."

He bit into one cautiously. I waited.

"Well, so what does it taste like?"

"Peanuts."

—Originally published March 2018

Author's Note: First Lady Rosalynn Carter, an activist and humanitarian to the end, died in November 2023. Her husband Jimmy remains in hospice care.

A
HUNGER
FOR
TOMATOES

**My cousin Edward Mitchell Seabrook Jr. was a shy man
with two passions.**

The first was science fiction. He would read it in his office
on Broad Street in Charleston, where he ostensibly sold real
estate and insurance. His pulp-novel overflow also crowded the
bookshelves in the second-floor bedroom I shared with my sister
Kaki during a grossly hot summer vacation at Edward's beach
house on Folly Island. Edward's mother was sister to my Nana, his
father cousin to my grandfather. As a teenager, lying next to a box
fan with a damp washrag on my forehead, I devoured paperbacks
with lurid cover art by Roy G. Krenkel and Frank Frazetta: *Tanar
of Pellucidar, Pirates of Venus, The Cave Girl.*

His other passion was tomatoes.

Because Edward's front yard on the Folly River was a sandy
coastal mess of prickly crabgrass and spartina, he positioned
50-gallon industrial drums, sawed in half, outside the kitchen
door. He grew tomatoes in tin cans but was a member of the
Agricultural Society of South Carolina. His seedlings raced up
poles in a mysterious soil mix about which he was tight-lipped.
As the sun burned off dew and the hour for lunch approached,
Edward lumbered down the rows checking ripeness until he
found a few about to crack with juice, and twisted the warm fruit

from its vine. The smell of tomato leaves fell somewhere on the spectrum between scorched tobacco and a mechanic's grease rag. The flavor of the tomatoes themselves, an excruciating alchemy of acidity and sugar, only he knew how to achieve. In the kitchen, one of my great-aunts or Edward's wife, Lucy, made sandwiches. I can't recall if the mayonnaise was Duke's, but the bread was squishy and white. I ate mine, bare feet dangling at the end of the dock, or in a rope hammock on the porch, with one of Edward's fantasies about mutant aliens inches from my nose.

Where would Southern culture be without the tomato?

. . .

One of the earliest references in Southern cookery appears in the private journals of Harriott Pinckney Horry of Hampton Plantation. By 1770, she was collecting receipts in a journal about life in the Santee River Basin, especially during the Revolution, when she managed the property alone. Her house served as a refuge for women and children fleeing the British occupation, and it was in her fields where Brigadier General Francis Marion, known as the Swamp Fox, hid when enemy troops arrived at her door to search for him. Horry's instructions "To Keep Tomatoos [sic] for Winter use" by stewing and storing in pint pots with melted butter as a sealant seems labor intensive to those of us equipped with modern refrigeration and access to hothouse varieties at the nearest Publix. Not only was it a hedge against a season of want, but also a pragmatic embrace of what the New World offered.

Since that early recipe, the tomato's appeal for Southerners became universal. Tomato aspic at church suppers. Tomato pie for picnics. Tomato gravy with cat-head biscuits. Tomatoes in succotash, chutney, puddings, and perloo. Green ones get their own dance party. An early version fried in "hot lard" appeared in the *Blue Grass Cook Book* by Minnie C. Fox, a collection of Kentucky recipes published in 1904 that acknowledged the vital role of Black cooks. In 1971, Helen Mendes updated the recipe in her soul-food classic *The African Heritage Cookbook*. Let's also thank novelist Fannie Flagg for indelibly commemorating those golden-crusted disks in *Fried Green Tomatoes at the Whistle Stop Café*.

But no one in the Southern culinary canon rivaled Ernest Matthew Mickler, who praised the Kitchen Sink Tomato Sandwich in *White Trash Cooking*:

"In the peak of the tomato season, chill 1 very large or 2 medium tomatoes that have been vine-ripened and have a good acidy bite to their taste. Take two slices of bread. Coat them with ¼ inch of good mayonnaise. On one piece of bread, slice the tomato ¼ inch thick. Salt and pepper that layer. Add another layer of sliced tomato, and again salt and pepper. Place the other piece of bread on top of this, roll up your sleeves, and commence to eat over the kitchen sink while the juice runs down your elbows."

Finding my way back to that sandwich took up most of a year.

TOMATL

"¿Qué es el trabajo?" Julia Perkins asked. "What's the job?"

A group of women facing her at the bulletin board repeated the English lesson in unison. On a Sunday afternoon in late April at the Coalition of Immokalee Workers (CIW) headquarters, members gathered for their weekly coffee klatch to learn a few handy phrases, trade day care schedules, and discuss the cost of groceries. Boxes of Polvorones and Canelitas cookies lay scattered on the folding table. A banda tune by Los Jefes de la Sierra Grande leaked from the sound booth of Radio Conciencia La Tuya next door. Murals depicting tomato workers in the field covered butter yellow walls. Hand-painted slogans "No Mas Abusos," "Comida Justa" and "Justice for Farmworkers" hung above a cluster of desks.

"What kind of work is it?" Perkins said. "What do I need to apply?"

Perkins, a CIW education coordinator born in North Carolina, ended her lesson, and the women rose to rearrange the folding chairs and put away the snacks. All dressed neatly in jeans, cotton tops, clean sneakers. Gold necklaces, pierced ears. Long hair pulled back in sensible ponytails or braids. Cell phones tucked back into purses. Many still worked in the fields; others were field agents for the Coalition. Nice ladies, all.

Bet you'd never guess they're expert hunger strikers.

. . .

Immokalee was ground zero for Florida's commercial tomato crop. Broad, flat fields lined the main road into town from the Gulf Coast, and on certain stretches, high chain-link fences prevented panthers from crossing the asphalt that cuts across their swampy Western Everglades habitat. Loaded tractor-trailers rumbled out of packinghouses. A pinhooker market in an open lot sold produce too ripe for long-distance shipping. A party store advertised piñatas, and bottles of Mexican Coke filled the cold drink case at Mr. Taco. Waitresses in bustiers and fishnet stockings circled gamblers hunched over slots at the Seminole casino. Street roosters waged turf wars in grassy ditches. Blue tarps still patched damaged roofs long after Hurricane Irma pummeled Florida. In an improvised courtyard between ramshackle mobile homes with boarded-up windows, little girls built sand castles in the dirt, pretending to be at the beach. One of their parents, who paid $60 a week to share the single-wide with up to eleven other occupants, mentioned that after the 2016 election, a few babies were named Melania.

Across the street from CIW headquarters, the parking lot at La Fiesta #3 grocery store served as a depot for the battered school buses that transported agricultural workers. They bought warm tortillas inside at crack of dawn each morning. When the buses returned at end of day, water coolers were dumped on the asphalt to evaporate in the still torrid heat. Many town residents commuted on bicycles, not due to a quaint civic ordinance but because they couldn't obtain a legal driver's license or afford car payments on a harvester's wage. In 1960, Edward R. Murrow reported from Immokalee on the harsh lives of Black migrant workers in the CBS documentary *Harvest of Shame*; since then, the town's population largely shifted to Latino and Haitian. Whatever change had taken place in the fields—as basic as access to shade and water, as critical as exposing wage theft and sexual harassment—was in great part due to Coalition activists.

Members of the CIW were fantastic at nonviolent resistance. One of their cornerstone initiatives was the Fair Food Program, a humane workplace monitoring collaboration with big ag companies including Gargiulo, Pacific Tomato, and Lipman Family Farms, and fast food giants McDonald's, Subway, and Chipotle. Walk through the produce aisle at Whole Foods or Trader Joe's and inspect the tiny green Fair Food seal on those clamshells of glossy grape tomatoes and genetically engineered slicers. It represented decades of toil and deprivation.

But the Fair Food seal can't be found at Publix or Wendy's.

Not yet.

. . .

The next day, Nely Rodriguez, a robust woman in her mid-50s, walked into the CIW offices and shook my hand. She wore a caramel-colored knit sweater over a tank top and capris. Rodriguez, originally from Tamaulipas, Mexico, spoke in a low alto.

"When I first came here, I picked apples and asparagus in Michigan," she said. "Then in Florida, tomatoes, squash, and eggplant; and since 2007, my work at the Coalition is organizing in the community, with the Sunday women's group, the radio, and labor-abuse investigations outside the Fair Food Program."

She also took part in hunger strikes. Her first fast was in 2012—a weeklong protest at Publix headquarters in Lakeland, Florida. Founded in 1930 by George R. Jenkins, Publix was the largest closely held regional supermarket chain in the South, with 1,377 stores and retail sales over $54 billion, so if you shopped for groceries anywhere between Alabama and Virginia, chances were good you bought tomatoes at a Publix, or Publix Sabor, themed stores catering to Hispanic Americans. The company's official position for not taking part in the Fair Food Program maintained the CIW campaign was a labor dispute between workers and suppliers, rather than a human-rights issue. Undeterred, Rodriguez traveled up to New York in late winter for a chilly "Freedom Fast" strike outside the Park Avenue offices of Wendy's billionaire board chairman Nelson Peltz.

• • •

We sat at a picnic table under a pergola behind the cinder-block building. Doves cooed on a tin rooftop. Breezes rustled the sabal palms.

"I've never fasted. How did you feel at the end?" I asked.

"To be honest, I thought it would be more difficult than it was," she said. "For the first or second day, I had headaches, was tired, but by the third day, I felt more full of energy, lighter, and wasn't hungry anymore. Taking on a fast like this, you know you're doing it for a just cause, and you've seen abuses in the community and you want them to stop."

"Was there a time in your past when you were hungry?" I asked.

"Sometimes, working in the fields back in Mexico, because you had to finish a job and you can't stop, you get hungry. But for days and days because food wasn't available, like the Freedom Fast? No. There were days when food was just tortillas and beans, but there always was something to eat."

"So the strike was a different kind of hunger?"

"During the fast, I found myself reflecting on the things I've seen, like the mothers here who have to get up extremely early to drop their kids off at day care or school, but under the Fair Food Program, that is no longer the case. If we can make this program expand, those things will .change. Those things come into your mind and you can power through. After five or six days you want to continue. The feedback you get, the support from the community, that encouragement helps you get through the more difficult parts, urges you on."

"What was the first thing you ate after?"

"To break the fast, we ate bread all together. Then, we celebrated at the Cathedral of Saint John the Divine. The bishop was there, they had mariachis, and an enormous spread. I served myself salad, rice with vegetables, butternut squash soup. And at the end tres leches cake with whipped cream on top. "

Rodriguez smiled.

"That tasted so good."

. . .

Angela Navarette bought the maroon lace curtains shading windows of a modest tan ranch—company housing owned by Lipman Family Farms, one of North America's largest field-tomato growers—in a subdivision known as Farm Workers Village, beyond Immokalee town center where sidewalks end.

"They make it look nice. More like home," she said.

Her husband, Ignacio Lopez, rested in an armchair, a straw cowboy hat tipped back on his head. The room was stuffy in late afternoon. Julia Perkins and I sat at the dining table covered with a floral-pattern vinyl cloth while her colleague, Gerardo Reyes, examined the faulty settings on the air conditioning unit. On the stove, a pot of pollo con mole bubbled. Lopez, seventy-six, grew up in Veracruz; Navarette, sixty-one, was born in Guerrero. Both were members of the Coalition. They met in Immokalee; each had children from other marriages living on both sides of the border. She got here first, to harvest lettuce in Belle Glade and corn in Indiana. A trafficker dropped him off in Tennessee. They shared the house in Immokalee with six more workers during the winter growing season, then followed the crop in summer to South Carolina and Virginia.

"We came because of necessity," Navarette said, her face darkening. "In Mexico, I was taking care of all the kids of my daughters and sons. One was studying to become a nurse, and so I tried to think of ways to support her, and coming here became an idea."

I asked Angela her full name.

"Hernandez-Navarette," she said. "But not the bad Navarettes. When I first got here, people at the company looked at me funny when I said my name, then I learned the story, but it still took a while to clear it up."

She referred to a notorious family of crew bosses that brutalized and enslaved twelve Hispanic tomato pickers, holding them captive and chained inside a box truck for almost two and a half years.

Navarette got up to stir the mole.

"Is there a special technique to working tomatoes?" I asked.

"It took me a month to learn," she said. "The crew leader told me it's really heavy work, and I felt uncomfortable taking a break all the time because everyone was looking at me, but Ignacio works really quickly, picking up the slack. He's a matador."

Reyes explained "matado" is slang for killer or badass, the fastest one who makes everyone else look bad.

"Even with my age, I love working in the fields," Lopez said. "I'm fast, they don't beat me. When I get tired, I am limping, my feet hurt, but I'm still out there. I'm fresh like lettuce."

"Do you concentrate on a tomato variety?"

"We pick tintos," Lopez said. "It's a little bit easier than picking greens, because with the greens, everyone moves so quickly, but with these, it's easier to spot because they're a little red."

A bucket of tintos sat on the kitchen floor, next to a five-gallon pickle tub and six-packs of Grape Crush. Navarette brought one to the table. It was about as ripe as a snow globe.

"How many buckets a day?" I asked.

"Around seventy-five," Lopez said. "Sometimes only twenty-five or thirty when there's not many left, but the piece rate for the reds is higher."

Each full bucket, or "piece," weighed thirty-two pounds. On a great day, that added up to 2,400 pounds hauled by hand to a field truck by a bow-legged septuagenarian shorter than me.

Reyes, passing around a plate of microwaved tortillas, remarked that harvesting the tinto used to be a niche market of pinteros, or pinhookers, who hired day labor not affiliated with an established crew and paid them cash.

Navarette served her pollo con mole next to generous scoops of rice mixed with dried green pigeon peas and stewed tintos. (She doesn't eat raw tomatoes.) Her sauce covering the chicken legs was nutty, mildly fiery, and had an elusive sweetness. In Nahuatl, it's called mōlli or chilmōlli. I wanted to bathe in it.

"If we see you in South Carolina, I will teach you how to make this," she said.

. . .

We get the word "tomato" from the Nahuatl language. The root word tomatl was adapted to tomate by the Spanish, and then the "e" distorted to "o" for English speakers. That subtle shift from consonant to vowel was a history of conquest, colonialism, and migration. Nahuatl was the Aztec language spoken in central Mexico, including the Navarette-Lopezes' home states of Guerrero and Veracruz, and was considered the prestige language of pre-Hispanic Mesoamerica. The wild ancestor of all tomatoes was *Solanum pimpinellifolium*, a resilient perennial with pea-sized fruit originating in northern Peru and southern Ecuador, with cousins appearing in climates as varied as the Atacama Desert and on the lower slopes of the Andes. The modern tomato, *Solanum lycopersicum*, took another 10,000 years to evolve, and while the date of domestication was unknown, it was cultivated by Aztecs around 500 BC. The tomato then dispersed on Spanish trade routes to Europe and Asia, Africa and the Caribbean, but unlike other New World botanical discoveries such as peanuts or corn, it was greeted with far deeper prejudice because it belonged to the poisonous nightshade family.

The earliest account of tomatoes grown in North America was found in herbalist William Salmon's *Botanologia* of 1710, although Spanish settlers likely introduced the plant to their colonies and missions on the southeast coast centuries earlier. Seeds may also have arrived through the Jamaica slave trade. In Louisiana, Cajun and Creole cooks adopted the tomato for gumbos and jambalayas. Elsewhere, bias continued into the nineteenth century. In 1836, S. D. Wilcox, editor of the *Florida Agriculturalist*, wrote after eating his first: "The tomato is an arrogant humbug and deserves forthwith to be consigned to the tomb of the Capulets." At the end of the century, the father of the modern commercial tomato, seed saver Alexander W. Livingston, achieved the varieties he named "Paragon" and "Acme" through generations of selective breeding. One hundred years more, too much hybridization—for shape, durability, color, disease, and drought resistance—had a singular unintended consequence. Tomatoes started tasting downright boring.

And that brings us to the flavorless globe, picked by migrant workers and reddened by ethylene gas in packinghouses before landing in supermarkets with callous public relations positions on labor practices.

I wouldn't grace that between two slices of bread.

Angela and Ignacio left in the night.

WOLF PEACH

"Let's take the golf cart," said Richard Blake "Bubba" Crosby Jr.

On a cloudless morning in late June, he climbed aboard a sky-blue Ford 3000 tractor and set out for his three-acre vegetable patch, a few hundred feet off the back porch of his house in Hardeeville, South Carolina. A tall man with thinning white hair and gnarled hands, the 91-year-old retired tomato farmer was a descendant of Charles Cotesworth Pinckney, a signer of the Declaration of Independence, and a distant cousin to Harriott Pinckney Horry. At one time, Crosby farmed 300 acres in rented fields strung on the coast between Hilton Head and Beaufort, before bridges connected the barrier islands on Port Royal Sound.

"I started farming when I got out the Army in '47," he said in a gravelly drawl. "I used my daddy's tractor and planted watermelons. We had to use a horse to side it up close, to work the crop itself, because tractors weren't too good then."

He also grew cotton, daffodils, rice, corn, soy, and velvet beans. Raised beef cattle. By the 1960s, he shifted into tomatoes, and for a year contracted to grow for the same company that employed Angela Navarette and Ignacio Lopez. That arrangement didn't work out.

"I learned how from nothing, started growing tomatoes because they was growing in Beaufort," Crosby said, shutting off the vintage 1965 tractor inside the electric deer fence. "Planted 20 acres the first time."

His property wrapped around a bend of the New River, not far north of Savannah on Oaktie Highway, between alligators in the marsh and rattlesnakes in the piney woods. Crosby and I strolled down three neat rows of staked vines, about a hundred feet long, heavy with fruit.

He bent down and moved leaves aside with his walking cane.

"You want to know how we plant those tomatoes to make 'em? Is that important? I fixed the ground like a month before time to plant, put a plow down about that deep right where the row is going, and it brings some clay up a little bit, softens the dirt, and I put fertilizer, 5-10-15 heavy potash, the length of those rows, a ten-quart bucket, there, one time. I put bagged lime down like the fertilizer, because the garden gets blossom-end rot, then wait a couple of weeks before planting the crop. They susceptible to everything, you know."

"What kind of tomatoes?" I asked.

He chuckled.

"The tomatoes that I plant, they come with a number on them, I get a few from a friend of mine who is in charge of the planting operation at 6Ls."

"So you're planting the same kind as Lipman?"

"They owe me plenty."

. . .

Southern farmers like Crosby could no longer compete against agricultural conglomerates with million-dollar tractors, acreage in multiple states, proprietary varieties, and experimental field-trial stations. Independent packinghouses, which once serviced smaller growers, also shuttered or merged.

We left the tractor in the field and returned to his cement porch, where he showed me a flat of scrawny seedlings reserved for fall. Red orbs, stem side down, ripened on a picnic table. Crosby settled himself in a rocking chair as his wife Joyce, eighty-six, came outside to offer bottles of cold water. They have been married for sixty-four years. A petite woman with downy hair, she still preserved broccoli, cabbage, collards, and corn from their garden, and had just finished canning sixty quarts of snap beans. We sat, rocking, to catch the breeze and recover from the direct sun.

"We old but we good," she said, smiling at her husband.

A mosquito hawk droned the porch.

"How many tomatoes do you get in a season?" I asked.

"We picked nine gallon buckets so far, but I've given away a bunch, and sell enough off the table to pay for the garden."

Joyce chimed in.

"Bubba just gave up Farm Bureau. He was on the school board, done a lot of community stuff, played softball until he was seventy-nine."

"When we got married in '54, there was local Blacks around here didn't have any work," she said. "And they all worked in his fields. We had a boy that started as a teenager, he was an alcoholic, and I fed him a big plate of dinner, ate everything we did."

"There was no welfare then," Crosby said. "Nobody had anything."

"How many workers on the farm?" I asked.

"I had two, sometimes three," he said.

"And when picking?"

"Two, three hundred."

"And where did all the pickers come from?"

"They were transit, same as they got in Beaufort now. We had a labor camp. When the season was over they'd go up the road."

• • •

The Crosbys' youngest daughter, Cheryl, pulled into the yard. A horse trainer and wild animal rehabber, she had a baby raccoon in a meshed pet carrier. She used to pick tomatoes for fun as a child and sold them out of the field.

"If we picked a bucket of tomatoes, that was our money. I'd spend it on junk food at the Nickel Pump gas station," Cheryl said, as the raccoon crawled into her arms and perched on her neck. "We'd go to the movies. He didn't pay us, but we went to private school."

She confessed a dislike for raw tomatoes.

"But I like salsa and ketchup and tomato sauce," she said, selecting unripe slicers from the table. "I'm getting these for someone who wants to make fried green tomatoes. Fresh out of the garden taste, it's a lot sweeter."

"Bubba, what's the best way to eat them?" I asked.

Crosby laughed.

"I eat them a little bit green. It don't have quite as much juice running down your arm."

"But what about a tomato sandwich?"

"I use Miracle Whip," Joyce said. "My mother used Hellmann's. You have to do what you want with the mayonnaise, and I peel the tomato and slice it regular. Salt, pepper would be good. We buy that Nature's Butter Bread. That's what he likes."

"Ugh," Cheryl said.

TRUE FRUIT

"The migrants are here."

I heard that at gas stations and convenience stores along Highway 21, when at the height of tomato picking season in South Carolina, the population ballooned on Port Royal Sound. (In the late sixteenth century, the settlement of Santa Elena, on Parris Island, was the capital for the Spanish colony of La Florida.) As in Immokalee, trucks hauled loads to packinghouses on the main road. Low-profile bodegas offered check cashing and international call services. Scarecrows in white hazmat suits and bilingual trespassing signs were posted at the entrance to the fields, shielded from view by high scrub. Outside the port town of Beaufort and the Marine Corps Recruit Depot, this region also remained rural. Here, the predominant culture was Gullah, with the community of Frogmore on Saint Helena Island a place of historic significance; all it takes is a turn onto Dr. Martin Luther King Jr. Drive to pass by the Penn School, where emancipated slaves first received a formal education in 1862 on a campus of whitewashed clapboard buildings.

Early on the morning of the summer solstice, the forecast for Saint Helena included a heat-index warning of 110 degrees. It remained cool enough under the shade trees as buses dropped off pickers at a labor camp. Laundry dried on lines outside one of the row houses, portable toilets sat under a carport shed, flatbed trucks stacked with empty dumper bins parked in the yard. The pickers headed first to a hand-washing station, and then jostled for seats at picnic tables. Most of them young men, wearing baseball caps, back braces, bandanas, work boots, cut off stretchable sleeves to protect forearms, their jeans stained muddy green on the knees. A few women scattered among the crews.

Crew bosses and ag company representatives also arrived.

"Hola, muchachos," said Gerardo Reyes.

The response was muted, polite.

. . .

The Coalition of Immokalee Workers conducted field sessions at farms that signed the Fair Food Program agreement, and during the season they traveled north along the same route as the migrants. Saint Helena was a regular stop. The session addressed rights and responsibilities of both workers and farmers: standard safety practices, tracking hours, and how to report discrimination or abuse. It took about an hour. That morning, the CIW activists worked through three sessions, with about 200 workers in all. As Reyes talked, Julia Perkins and Nely Rodriguez handed out brochures. Other staff held up murals painted on plastic tarps to illustrate key points. One had an outsize cartoon sun burning above a row of vines, and Reyes commented that on really hot days, all you saw was that big yellow orb. The crews laughed.

The mood shifted when Nely Rodriguez took her turn to talk about sexual harassment, standing next to a mural of two workers commenting on a female picker's appearance as she bent over in a field. Some men snickered, looking nervously at each other for support.

"What if this was your mother or sister?" she asked.

That same morning, Melania Trump had left the White House for Andrews Air Force Base, en route to an unannounced humanitarian visit with detained immigrant children and unaccompanied minors at a shelter in a Texas border town. She wore a $39 olive green Zara jacket with the words "I REALLY DON'T CARE, DO U?" printed in faux graffiti on the back.

Neither do many tomato producers. According to Farmworker Justice, a nonprofit advocacy group in Washington, DC that addressed immigration policy for migrant and seasonal workers, more than half of America's two million farmworkers were undocumented and marginalized. And despite the CIW's outreach, this still engendered an environment where unscrupulous employers, from crew bosses in the field on up to white collars in corporate offices, needed to be held accountable for illegal or deficient practices to get their crops to market.

. . .

When tomato pickers migrated with the crop, their crew bosses sent a truck ahead to transport bare necessities. Personal microwaves and wall-unit air conditioners. Chairs. Storage tubs filled with clothing, linens, pots and pans. Angela Navarette packed chilies because she couldn't find the right variety for her mole in South Carolina. For the season there, she and Ignacio Lopez were assigned to a rented house with seven other workers, a prefab double-wide set back from the road leading toward Land's End on Saint Helena. Cots for the bachelors crammed the living room, but the kitchen made Navarette happy as she preferred it to more basic quarters in the labor camps.

We stood at the sink as she cut up two chickens. She fried plantains in a pan. Then garlic and onion, peanuts, raw pumpkin seeds, raisins, and sesame. Ground together cloves, cumin, cinnamon. She chopped two large field tomatoes in a blender with toasted chiles and broth from the stewing chickens.

"My secret ingredient," she said, her dark eyes brightening. "I thought this one up myself. Galleta de animalito."

Animal crackers.

The smashed cookies made the sauce intensely personal.

She stopped stirring the pot to check laundry soaking in a bucket outside on a porch next to a dead refrigerator. An all-day job to get tomato stains out of her clothes.

"Old house, old bath, old clothes. But it's all going to be clean."

"What do you wear?" I asked.

"A long-sleeve blouse, shirt over that. Some people use lots of bandanas, but I put one under my baseball cap. Any other hat gets in the way of the bucket. In Mexico, all the campesinos would use a sombrero."

Cicadas buzzed in the woods.

"When you're picking tomatoes, your hands get stained and dirty," Navarette said.

"How do you get it off?"

"You take a tomato and break it open and rub on like soap, and then the stain comes out when you wash your hands."

• • •

The chicken took three hours to cook down, and despite air conditioning on full blast, the kitchen grew uncomfortably steamy. I asked Navarette how she abided in the summer weather. She dug around in the refrigerator and pulled out a liter bottle of pineapple-flavored Suero Oral electrolyte solution. (Suero means serum in Spanish.) The caution label recommended use for severe dehydration caused by diarrhea, vomiting, or excessive perspiration.

"Nobody trusts the water on the truck. Who knows where it comes from? I drink this instead."

Lopez parked a pickup in the yard and came inside. He sat down and pulled up his pant legs to show me his knees, the joints swollen, inflamed, possibly arthritic. He kept rubbing them. Lopez explained he'd been to a free clinic for medicine and x-rays, but the doctors thought he might need an operation. Two months before, when I met him in Florida, he was still in the fields. Now, he cleaned crew quarters.

A matado no longer.

"Not a lot of tomatoes right now," he said. "It's not a good year. The cold impacted the crop here, and the rain, too. We used to get checks of $400 a week. There have been seasons when Angela was paid $1,000 in a single check. But now, every week we've been here, it's about $140."

"How do you live on that amount? How can you afford groceries?"

They looked at each other.

"We are worried about what will come next."

"After eighteen years, I'm tired," said Navarette, her lined face sadder. "I want to go home. Ignacio wants to go back to Veracruz, but I would like to be in Guerrero again."

"We are living in a country that's not ours," Lopez said. "We struggle with that. We think about how one day to the next everything could change, and how many people have been taken away. You have to be resilient. We need to not let our passions get the best of us. Just endure."

Navarette served lunch, the mole even better than last time.

"If we see you in Virginia, I will teach you tamales," she said.

TOMMATUH

The next day, Howard Chaplin pumped gas opposite me at the Sunoco on Sea Island Parkway. A slim man with wire-rim glasses and curly white sideburns, he politely wished me a good morning in a Gullah accent. I looked closer at his pickup truck, with a jumble of empty crates in the cab.

"Are those crab traps, sir?"

"Vegetable bins. Been up to the food bank in Yemassee with a load of my tomatoes."

I stepped over the median to shake his hand.

Those born on the sea islands had reason to be wary of people from off, especially real estate developers. This led to a damaging misconception that Gullah culture was dying. Far from true. Without the rich heritage of language, music, and cooking of the Gullah Geechee, descendants of the first Africans to toil here, the Lowcountry would be a poorer place altogether. Harriott Pinckney Horry enslaved workers in her fields and kitchen; she certainly wasn't out there growing or preserving the tomatoes that appeared in her journals. We wouldn't have most of the dishes that came after, either.

Before retirement, Chaplin, seventy-three, was a civilian employee of the US Marine Corps on Parris Island, and then a brick mason at Hunter Army Airfield. With his wife Harriet, a nurse and day care operator, Chaplin owned a country store on Storyteller Road, a byway between the leased fields and labor camps on Saint Helena. They sold dry goods and snacks to the Frogmore community, although later in the afternoon when I turned up there, a sign in the window advertised live crabs, and bushel baskets of fresh-picked okra sat on the floor near the refrigerator case. His T-shirt and glasses splattered with pluff mud, Chaplin returned with shrimp in his cast nets from the creeks feeding Port Royal Sound. Unflustered, he took me out back to look at his own fields, 20 acres surrounded by mature pecan trees. He also grew squash, broccoli, collard greens, and corn. What didn't sell in the store got donated for hunger relief. Yemassee was the nearest distribution center for the Lowcountry Food Bank network.

"How many rows of tomatoes?" I asked.

"I don't got too much, about sixteen rows here and ten rows there," he said. "Nothing big, just to keep me active."

"Have you been farming long?"

"I been doing this since knee high."

"How long has your family been here?"

"Oh, hoo! Quite a few years. About a hundred years back. Most of my folks, grandparents, from Cedar Grove. That's right on the island, too. The rest of them I don't know. We go back, we don't know where. We say 'longa go wit all that.'"

Chaplin had a limp, so we took our time between the rows of tomatoes, a few here and there on the ground rotting, weeds taking over the sandy soil. Chaplin explained he tested every other year, taking samples to CREC for advice on pesticides and fungicides. He let me pick a few red ones off the vines to take away. Chaplin pulled out a handkerchief and wiped his forehead.

"See those greens, that brown ring on it? I got to get them before they start ripening up. I done pick them twice this week, haven't watered in about two days. So hot."

Clouds piled up on the horizon as the sun dipped below the palmettos.

"Most of time you see rain all around in a circle, not a drop here. I ain't going to complain, we still have it good compared to other places."

"That's for sure," I said. "How do you eat a tomato?"

"I eat it natural, put a little ranch on it, slices of cucumber, that make a meal right there."

We headed back to his truck.

"I don't know why we grew so much this year, golly. I'm waiting for the kids to decide they want to take over. Had six, four still living. I probably give it up next year. Time bring on changes, right."

Chaplin gestured toward the distant rumble of tractors.

"I'm a peanut, just a little peanut to what they plant."

On leaving Saint Helena, I stopped at a stand closer to Beaufort owned by another Gullah farmer and bought extra tomatoes—pretty good slicers as it turned out—for dinner with my cousins in Charleston. Behind the bins holding cabbage and peaches was an acre-long hoop shed where a Hispanic worker sorted seedlings. He looked up and waved. Then, as I hesitated over a display of canary melons, face flushed, he took the tomatoes out of my arms and handed me a slice of the cooling melon.

"Es mejor, muy delicioso."

My car smelled of rind and kindness and tears.

LOVE APPLE

"I guess we kinda like to grow the funky stuff," Matthew Horry said.

A husky man with unruly brown hair, he leaned over a dog crate topped with propagation trays holding lumpy, wrinkled, unloveable tomatoes in the Chaparral RV camper he and his partner, Ashley Loponte, temporarily occupied on a rural lot outside Walterboro, South Carolina. Horry, 31, was a biological science technician who specialized in landrace and heirloom seed increase for the US Vegetable Lab at CREC. His personal pursuit was a half-acre organic plot of experimental tomatoes. The couple called their land Kindlewood Farms, their expansion dream after selling a starter home and backyard garden of two raised beds.

Their hothouse was a repurposed trampoline. A wine cooler served as a storage unit for ripe produce. They favored compost and fish emulsion over pesticides and fungicides. Their dog Gordon, a bouncy Labrador-pit bull mix, deterred critters as much as the electric fencing.

Loponte opened the camper door, letting in the heat and light of early July. Her cars keys hung from cotton-knit jalapeños with googly eyes.

"I like your key chain."

"That's her passion," Horry said. "Mine's tomatoes, and hers is peppers. We're a *Solanaceae* family."

"Before we closed on the land, we were at my mom's house, so I started a whole bunch of things without Matt's consent in the garage," Loponte said. "That's why everything is super early this year. We're the first to bring heirlooms to the market because I had to get motivated."

"It's a shared passion," Horry said. "A consuming passion."

On weekends, they sold at farm markets in the greater Charleston area. Horry obsessed over the catalog from Southern Exposure Seed Exchange, which preserved some of the South's rarest varieties, including "Aunt Lou's Underground Railroad Tomato," from original seed stock reportedly carried by an unnamed man who crossed to freedom from Kentucky.

"The heirlooms we have are Martha Washington, Amish Paste, Radiator Charlie's Mortgage Lifter, Striped German, Red Zebra, Black Cherry, Valencia, Solar Flare," Horry said, sorting through the flats. "We fought about this a lot. Tried to scale it down this year, keep only a few varieties."

He shrugged, acknowledging his inability to resist planting weirdos. "The homegrown tomato is something that piqued my interest. It's one of those vegetables, if you're fortunate to grow up eating them from the garden, you'll not be satisfied with the supermarket kind." He picked up a mottled yellow and purple tomato and handed it to me.

"We have a whole row from breeder Bradley Gates. These are called Blue Berry. They're not heirloom, but they are open pollinated. It's a little bitter when not fully ripe, but still gorgeous. The word heirloom, that's been overused. What I'm looking for is flavor and character."

I took a bite.

Like tomato pop rocks blowing up in my mouth.

Sadly, not sized for a sandwich.

Horry cut a juicy slice of Cherokee Purple. Only a devoted gardener could love this ugly bruise from Tennessee, also saved from extinction by happenstance and amateur breeders. Right then, I stopped looking for a slicer that would do justice to Ernest Matthew Mickler's kitchen sink recipe. It had a tingly balance of sweetness and acidity, a flavor that made me want to shout, "Roll up your sleeves."

He sold me one for $2.

"So, hey, wait a minute. Are you related to the Santee Horrys?" I asked.

He nodded.

"I'm a descendant."

"Okay, that's crazy. I'm related to Francis Marion."

Loponte looked bewildered at the two of us, grinning ancestry geeks.

"Our ancestors fought together in the Revolution," I said.

ARROGANT HUMBUG

Not long ago, I bumped into my cousin Edward Seabrook's widow, Lucy, on the street in Charleston. Folly was no longer a sleepy buffer island. She still owned the beach house but was deeding it to one of her nieces.

"What happened to Edward's books?" I asked.

She winced, and then shrugged, apologetically.

"Oh, we threw them out."

At the end of that childhood vacation, I snitched *The Prince of Peril* and *Thuvia, Maid of Mars*, and stuffed them in my suitcase hoping Edward wouldn't miss a few paperbacks from his collection. (He probably did.) They still sat on shelves in a spare bedroom in my house. Edward Seabrook's formula for a great tomato, however, was lost to the ages.

While we now have so many other fanciers, seed savers, scientists, and botanists working on reviving the flavor of the slicer, we remain deeply compromised in our hunger for a fair— and fairly decent-tasting—tomato. The Coalition for Immokalee Workers has collaborated with the Student/Farmworker Alliance on other actions to boycott Wendy's. Publix remains a Fair Food Program holdout.

Before Edward Seabrook went to the garden beyond, it occurred to me to ask about his mystery soil mix. He could transform my abrupt, gender-bending name into a soft, elegant crescendo, resonating on the scale between Howard Chaplin and Bubba Crosby. I loved hearing Edward talk. Few people alive still had that accent. It also meant I didn't always catch everything he said. He mumbled a series of numbers, some mutant formula, and thinking about it, I wonder if it was the heavy phosphate favored by Crosby.

Then again, Edward could have been speaking Martian, for all I know.

— Originally published September 2018

Author's Note: Angela Navarette and Ignacio Lopez, whose names were changed to protect their identities, returned to Immokalee when the planting cycle started again. Bubba Crosby died in 2023.

AN
UNDESERVED
GIFT

My mother knew two okra recipes. She would fry the chopped pods in cornmeal. Almost edible, because fried. The other dish was from her childhood, the one she ate on still summer afternoons at her grandmother's house in Columbia, South Carolina. Stewed okra and tomatoes for the midday dinner prepared by a cook named Addie.

Addie had a lumbering gait. She wore a china-blue uniform and a heavily starched white apron secured with a wide sash knotted in a butterfly bow. Behind a swinging door shielded by a folding screen, her kitchen contained a large work table that held her staples and spices. Pots hung from hooks, pans stacked on a shelf beneath. A gas stove with porcelain petcocks had to be coaxed into flame with wooden matches. A sink with a drain board where she washed produce purchased by my great-grandmother, Mary Cunningham Shane, who drove her Packard to a farm market on Saturday mornings before the heat of the day with my mother in tow. Sunburned farm women sold boxes of figs, watermelons, ears of corn. Bees hovered over the cantaloupes. Hens squawked in crates. My great-grandmother, in a linen dress and Panama hat, moved from stall to stall, truck to truck, inspecting the ripeness of tomatoes and the fragrance of peaches. Shelled butter beans measured into a tin quart container and okra weighed in a dangling scale. Women facing one another across laden tables, each keen to her responsibility, money tight during the Depression, mouths fixed to hard lines and harder bargains.

Every day, at five minutes after two, Addie rang a silver dinner bell. My mother washed her hands and prompted curls into order before standing next to her chair at the oval table in the high-ceilinged dining room. A covered dish of rice and a gravy boat rested next to the meat platter at her grandfather's hand. He carved while Addie elbowed through the pantry door and circled the table with her vegetables.

My mother said she would not have learned how to cook okra those two ways without Addie.

Hard truths lurked behind this sentimental memory passed down to me. Both dishes were tied to the Columbian Exchange, the cross-oceanic trade of ingredients that introduced the greater world to corn and tomatoes. As Jessica Harris wrote in *Iron Pots & Wooden Spoons*: "Okra is Africa's gift to New World Cooking." But both dishes would also not be possible without the Middle Passage, the other trade that transported millions into bondage.

Green snot, hacked from the back of the sinuses in the final stage of a bad head cold, swimming in a bloodbath.

SEEDS IN HER HAIR

No one can say who carried the first okra pods across the Atlantic. The location of origin was also obscure and its lineage unclear. Botanists squabbled for centuries over okra's classification, finally settling on *Abelmoschus esculentus*, from the Arabic abu-l-mosk, or father of musk, and a Latin root word for delicious, full of food. A member of the *Malvaceae*, or mallow, family, kissing cousins with cotton, cocoa, durian, and hibiscus. When the pods got too big and fibrous, okra took on the characteristics of its inedible relative balsa wood. Some botanists think okra came out of the Ethiopian

Highlands, then spread across the Arabian Peninsula and onward to the Indian subcontinent on two principal trade routes known as the Monsoon Exchange. To add to the confusion, indigenous edible mallows also grew in India, China, and Southeast Asia. The first located and unique mention of okra came to us through Moorish explorer Ahmad bin Muhammad bin Mufarrij bin Abdillah, a descendant of freed slaves whose *Botanical Journey*, published in 1216, was an early book on plant and herb species based on his observations in the field. He was a teacher of fellow botanist Ibn al-Baitar, who quoted his mentor in a later work about a preparation of tender okra cooked with meat in Egypt. He wrote: "By nature it is cold and moist—the moistest of all vegetables. The blood produced from it is bad. It is of little nutritive value. It is said to agree with people with a hot temperament. Its harmful effects are averted if it be eaten with a lot of hot spices."

Language is more telling about okra's exodus. Òkụrụ (Igbo), okro, ochroes, okree. Ila (Yoruba), nkruma (Twi), kingumbo (Bantu), quillobo (Congolese), quingumbo (Portuguese). Gombo (French), kalalou gombo (Haitian Creole). Baamiyaa (Arabic), bhindi (Hindi), tindisha (Sanskrit). The Fon people called it fevi. Sunn m'Cheaux, the resident Gullah lecturer in the African Language Program at Harvard University, explained that okra was a loanword, carried here phonetically, not in writing. Okra did not appear on ship provision manifests, unlike horse beans, cassava, or yams, the most common rations fed to enslaved Africans during voyages to the New World.

And yet, here it is.

. . .

The oldest African dish in seventeenth century Portuguese Brazil settlements was a spicy stew called carurú, made with smoked fish or shrimp, quiabo (okra), onions, palm oil, and peppers. It was almost identical to Senegalese soupou kanja and Nigerian ila asepo. Cou-cou was an okra and cornmeal dish eaten in Barbados. In Haiti, boiled breadfruit with okra sauce was called tomtom ak kalalou gombo. A fleeting reference to "un gombeau" appeared in a court document dated September 4, 1764, in the deposition of an enslaved woman named Comba by the French Superior Council of New Orleans. It may be the earliest mention in Louisiana. Less than a year later, Acadian leader Joseph "Beausoleil" Broussard arrived by way of Haiti with almost 200 French Canadian exiles.

Thomas Jefferson recorded the cultivation of okra in 1782, while the earliest published recipe was credited to Mary Randolph in *The Virginia Housewife*, and signposted a possible entry point with "Gumbo, a West India Dish." She also included the first method for "stewed ochra and tomatos" (sic). Sarah Rutledge came fast on her heels with "Okra Soup" in *The Carolina Housewife*, and the first recipe for a gumbo with okra from southern Louisiana appeared with the publication of Lafcadio Hearn's *La Cuisine Creole* in 1885. About its preparation, he advised: "Keep one vessel sacred to soup." Five years later, *The Picayune's Creole Cook Book* listed many okra dishes, including Gombo Fevi and Fevi Sauté à la Creole, a classy way of saying stewed okra and tomatoes. It was not a coincidence Creole recipes used the same word for okra as the Fon, who made up a large percentage of enslaved people brought to Louisiana in the early eighteenth century.

That was the mostly white timeline of okra's arrival on our shores. The Black narrative was oral, and this is where crop introduction took a fanciful turn. It also infuriated culinary historians who decried perpetuation of the "magical Negro cook" toiling in a hot kitchen for her mistress. In the Caribbean and South America, this foundation lore was applied to ackee and rice, particularly a version persistent to the Maroons of Suriname involving an escaped slave named Paánza, but the same tale also cropped up about okra and always centered on a woman of African heritage hiding precious seeds in her hair and delivering them from ship to subsistence plot—the kitchen gardens historian Judith Carney referred to as "the shadow world of cultivation."

The story took on mythic stature, the fecund heroine conveying sustenance on a terrifying journey, and into a hellish world where familiar dishes from the homeland empowered and strengthened, even unto resistance and freedom.

Nowhere in the South was this tale more persistent than New Orleans.

GUMBO YA YA

"Do you know what gumbo means?" asked Ricky Paul Breaux.

His bicycle lacked rubber tires, and he pushed it along on the steel rims, grinding to a stop next to the communal table where the Reverend Hannah Nielsen Quick and gardener Brooke Bullock arranged place settings. Caught off guard, the two young women looked up at him, puzzled. When they didn't give him the right answer, Breaux set down an insulated lunch bag, wiped his graying beard and shifted into Cajun French. "I was raised in the garden, and my mama would say: 'Va me chercher du gombo.'"

Okra Abbey was a "giving garden" behind a charter school on the corner of Hickory and Eagle streets, two blocks away from the Sewerage & Water Board treatment facility. Fresh food insecurity was high in this part of Pigeon Town, a historically Black working class neighborhood in the Seventeenth Ward. A couple of corner stores sold po'boys and fried chicken platters to go, but that's about it within walking distance, so this Presbyterian mission brought welcome greenery to a part of New Orleans still pockmarked by Katrina. A circle of flowers and herbs growing at the entrance was called the Gumbo Pot. Inspirational signs about faith and food hung on chain link fencing. Raised beds bordered with cinder blocks rested on asphalt paving, one of the most hostile environments for growing things when the heat bounced or the rain crashed down.

"There's nowhere for the water to go, so we get flooded with every storm," Bullock said. "And it would be great to grow in the ground. Everything was dead when we got here, and all the beds sky high with weeds."

She rose to help Breaux, who had wandered off to shovel compost. When lucid, he washed dishes or pulled weeds.

I turned to Reverend Quick.

"Tell me about the name?" I asked.

"Well, okra is one of the key ingredients here in New Orleans," she said. "And historically an abbey is a place of refuge to care for the poor and the young. The whole neighborhood is my congregation that I have been called to serve."

A native Californian, Quick left seminary in 2016 and landed in New Orleans. Instead of a pulpit, she had a tool shed. On occasions that called for her to dress formally as a pastor, the 26-year-old redhead wore a dog collar and bright green stole with two okra pods stitched like a cross, but she preferred ripped jeans and a T-shirt on weekdays when Okra Abbey opened its gates for a free midday meal called Grace & Greens.

"We try to identify folks who need food in the area," Quick said. "The corner stores don't even sell peanut butter."

When the garden first opened, in 2016, it was imagined as a community project where residents would plant their own seeds. That model, Quick explained, didn't work, but they found that people used the space in other ways. Sometimes, just to take a nap on the patio swing chair. Play chess. Meditate. Mural artist Henry Lipkis painted a river winding through the block-long plot that ended in a labyrinth. He also sprayed biblical graffiti on the vegetable beds. Christ with loaves and fishes on the Mount. The Last Supper. Cajun Adam and Eve picking fruit in a swampy Garden of Eden teeming with alligators.

. . .

As noon approached, more people arrived on bicycles or by foot, and helped themselves to pink plastic cups of ice water from a stadium cooler. A young couple with a toddler living in a renovated house across the street. A widower who didn't cook for himself. A middle-aged woman explained that she came for the Word, and stayed for the food. Two cooks carried hotboxes from a car parked outside the gates. A restaurant in the Garden District donated the meal, making use of the produce grown by Bullock. Turnips, cucumbers, radishes, eggplant, leeks, tomatoes, corn, and peppers. Basil and thyme. The obligatory okra. Any harvest that didn't go into the weekly meal got bundled into sacks and delivered to Pigeon Town's homebound the next day.

Quick and her volunteers served plates of baked chicken and vegetarian shepherd's pie. Salad greens from the garden were passed. She welcomed the eighteen people seated at the makeshift table and offered a brief benediction, head bowed, citing the first letter of the apostle Paul, 1 Corinthians 13.

"Paul says that there are different kinds of gifts but the same spirit distributes them. There are different kinds of service, but the same Lord. There are different kinds of working, but in all of them and in everyone, it's the same God at work. We're all blessed in different ways, and we all kind of bring that to the table as a community."

The meal ended quickly, but people lingered in the shade. Breaux leaned on a walking stick fashioned from creeper vine. A pile of chicken bones rested on his plate. Born in Assumption Parish, he lived a few blocks away but sometimes slept rough over by the Riverbend. He unzipped his lunch bag and pulled out bundles wrapped in facial tissue. Gently pulling apart layers, he revealed bars of soap carved with his pocket knife into fleurs de lys and turtles. Twin baby alligators, one with a bow around its neck, smelling like Irish Spring.

Breaux pointed at the gators.

"He got goo-goo eyes."

"What did your mother grow in her garden?" I asked, handing back the carving.

"We grew okra, we saved our seeds."

"And what did she cook?"

"Well, cherie," he said. "You can make a gumbo outta anything."

A POT OF GOO

"Okra will grow in Hell."

Timmy Perilloux tossed a plastic bag filled with pods into a hanging scale at his Crescent City Farmers Market stall on Carondelet Street early Saturday morning.

"They don't like cold weather," he said. "But once you get them up, they will grow and bear, every day, every day, every day."

Perilloux, a retired oil refinery worker, farmed in St. Charles Parish, west of the city, deep in Acadiana. He started with a pumpkin patch, and then got into Creole tomatoes and a few other crops. He wasn't sure about the variety grown in his fields, but he had been saving okra seeds for thirty years, and before that his uncle did the same. I asked how he cooked it. He paused between customers holding out dollar bills.

"Oh, listen. I plow the ground, I plant the seeds, I fertilize them. I cultivate them. I pick them. I'd be damned if I'm cooking them too. But Cracker Barrel got pretty good fried okra."

With my bag of okra in hand, I walked to the French Quarter for a quiet morning in the reading room at the Williams Research Center, which had an extensive collection of early Louisiana plantation records and family papers on microfiche. The staff attendant at the front desk noticed my purchase, and pointed me toward the lockers for safekeeping.

"You know our ancestors came here with okra seeds in their hair?"

"Who told you that?"

He smiled.

"People in New Orleans have always told that story. It's been around forever."

The day before, a local radio host snapped at me in a cookbook store for trying to track this down.

"Don't spread that awful story!" she said. "Haven't those people suffered enough?"

· · ·

The Williams Research Center's papers included a menu dated April 13, 1886, referencing gumbo, from a course on domestic arts at Straight University, established by the American Missionary Association as an institution of higher learning for African Americans. I also found a Depression-era label for the Tabasco brand's canned whole okra and tomatoes, a photograph of okra in the French Market dated 1936, and more recent images of Arthur J. "Mr. Okra" Robinson, one of the last singing street vendors who sold produce from his truck. He died in 2018.

By midafternoon, people gathered on the street to pay last respects to the musician who wrote "Gris-Gris Gumbo Ya Ya." At the corner of Basin and Canal, I waited with hundreds more as the glass-sided hearse drawn by a pair of horses, one black and one white, rolled by, bearing the Night Tripper home. Malcolm John Rebennack Jr.—Dr. John—once gave me a hug in Galatoire's Restaurant while I was in town reporting on the relief effort in St. Bernard Parish after the BP oil spill, and so I walked a little ways toward St. Louis Cemetery No. 1 with his coffin and second line. The Kinfolk Brass Band played "Li'l Liza Jane."

Still hanging onto the bag of okra, I caught a ride to Violet, out beyond the Lower Ninth Ward in St. Bernard Parish, and to get there, crossed over outflow canals and along roads next to levees that held back the Mississippi, a disconcerting vantage point as tankers floated at an elevation higher than the car roof. Passed the field where the Battle of New Orleans was decided, and Andrew Jackson became a national hero. Not much farther, the river drained into the gulf, but not before a whole lot of alligators occupied a whole lot of bayou. The storm surge from Katrina hit hardest here. Pretty much everyone who didn't evacuate died, and just as the parish was recovering, the oil spill happened, another kick in the teeth to the shrimpers and refinery workers and farmers and hourly wage earners at the Walmart Superstore.

. . .

Betty Funches gave me such a look when I didn't chop the holy trinity fine enough to suit her.

"Get out my kitchen!" she joked.

She attacked the celery, bell peppers, and onions with a small knife until satisfied. The pre-K teacher learned to cook gumbo from her mother. One of seventeen children, she also baked OoeyGooey and 7-Up cakes for celebrations in the neighborhood. Her father drove a truck for National Food Company but also farmed four fields in Violet.

"He had a little farmer truck going around selling zucchini, squash, mustard greens. Okra, he sold it to Circle Food Store. It looked like this kind. This is Creole okra, you can tell because it got these lines."

She indicated the smooth ridges that ran from stem to tip. Funches picked through the bag of okra from Timmy Perrilloux, looking for the freshest pods, then trimmed them and threw the rounds into a skillet for browning.

"See that slime coming through? That's where the grease been pulling it out."

"How can you tell when okra is fresh?" I asked.

"My daddy taught me," she said, holding out a firm pod. "If I can't cut through it, means it's too hard and you can't cook it. If the seeds be real big, then the okra gone to seed, and my daddy would let them dry and replant them."

She wiped slime off her hands and stirred together Golden flour and corn oil. Her Creole accent made oil sound like "earl." She called roux "brown gravy." Didn't believe in the tradition of stirring it with a wooden spoon, said hers would come out "just fine." When running short on time, she confessed to putting a little Zatarain's in her roux.

"That's my cheat," she said, grinning. "All good cooks cheat."

Funches chopped up skinned chicken thighs and hickory-smoked sausage, and tested the rice in another pot simmering on the stove. Diced Creole tomatoes. Her youngest daughter Jighra, a 10-year-old with long micro-braids, fetched more bowls and knives from next door. A dog barked in the backyard. The neighbors had returned from crabbing down in Delacroix. She dropped crabs one by one into a slow boil, and they expired barely struggling, turning from bluish gray to traffic-cone orange. She flipped up the back shells and removed the gills, and then cracked them down the middle. When the trinity finished sautéing in the sausage grease, Funches put everything into her stockpot except the crabs and okra.

"Do you know how okra got here?" I asked.

"No."

I lost track of the seasonings. Salt, pepper, garlic powder, a jumble of spices. She pulled jar after jar from the cupboard, poured in handfuls, stirred, tasted, and added more.

"Gumbo is just whatever you want to put in there."

Before Katrina hit, Funches evacuated to Houston with her mother. It was the first time she left for any storm. The flood topped the roof of her ranch house, and her family lost everything. They stayed away for two years in a rented apartment with an electric stove, and she kept burning things. Her oldest son still lived in Texas, but she came back to renovate in Violet. Jighra was her change baby.

She finally added the crabs and okra. Funches wiped her glasses, steamy from stirring the thickening soup. Her daughter went outside to play until dinner.

"Don't let anybody know I'm cooking okra gumbo," she yelled.

MANJELWA

"Be food for one another."

The Soulful Voices choir at Saint Augustine Cathedral belted out this refrain on St. John's Eve. They sounded more tent revival than Catholic mass. Or maybe an early-to-rise jazz session. Keeping the faith didn't have to mean keeping it solemn, and as the Reverend Emmanuel Malenga gave a homily about the Eucharist, the congregation murmured their amens and hallelujahs.

"Come to the feast, sustain us in our daily lives," he preached.

A handsome church two blocks north of Rampart Street in Faubourg Tremé, Saint Augustine was famous for the War of the Pews. Established in 1842 by free people of color, who also bought side pews for the enslaved, they outbid white parishioners vying for the age-worn wooden seating that remained in place to this day. A tomb on church grounds, dedicated to an unknown slave, hung with chains and shackles. I sat in a pew at the back, where the acoustics were better, and found a little refuge. A good way to bookend a day that would conclude in an entirely different ceremony singular to this city.

Or, as manbo Sallie Ann Glassman said, "It feels good to cool our heads in these traumatic days."

St. John's Eve appeared on the Gregorian calendar next to the Solstice in late June. Unlike other saint days commemorating martyrdom, this one celebrated the birth of John the Baptist.

It was also the holiest day in the Louisiana Vodou calendar. The first account of St. John's Eve in New Orleans appeared in the

Commercial Bulletin on July 5, 1869: "June is the time devoted by the Voodoo worshippers to the celebration of their most sacred and therefore most revolting rites. Midnight dances, bathing and eating, together with less innocent pleasures, make the early summer a time of orgies for the blacks."

Other newspapers of the period printed sensationalized accounts with tropes about race and faith. Despite this, Marie Laveau, the original "Voodoo Queen of New Orleans", was largely responsible for popularizing the celebration with bonfires at the place where Bayou St. John drained into Lake Pontchartrain. A devout Catholic, she was also known for her charity work, attending to yellow fever victims and reportedly bringing gumbo to condemned prisoners as a last meal. She spoke "Gombo French." A hairdresser by profession, Laveau is portrayed wearing a tignon, the knotted headdress required of enslaved Creole women. Any altar to her memory contains hair accessories. Pins, barrettes, combs, ribbons.

Sallie Ann Glassman erected an altar for Laveau every Midsummer night on Bayou St. John. She was a Vodou priestess for the modern age. A vegan. Wore spring-loaded jogging heels. Climbed Kilimanjaro. Born Jewish in Maine, she heard the calling in New Orleans, and initiated in Haiti. Her house of worship, Achade Meadows, was in a blind alley decorated with graffiti art of the loa, Vodou spirits, squeezed between Piety and Desire in the Bywater. Her weekly ceremonies had as much to do with interpretive art as summoning the invisibles and honoring the ancestors.

"People refer to Vodou as a kind of gumbo religion because it takes on these other influences that are blended together," Glassman told me before the ceremony started. "A lot like ingredients in a gumbo where the spices remain distinct, but it becomes another dish different from what you started with. It's so fluid and expressive."

An artist who worked in pastels and oils, Glassman often portrayed Laveau opening a curtain beaded with cowrie shells that shields a darkened room, inviting viewers into an unknown space.

"Vodou gave people the power to endure slavery and to transform horrible experiences into strengths and creative genius," she said. "That ability to draw on an invisible power that didn't bend to earthly powers was certainly very reassuring for enslaved people, and terrifying for slave owners."

...

A southerly wind blew as celebrants dressed in cooling white gathered at dusk on a neutral ground between the water and Esplanade Avenue, closer to Magnolia Bridge than the outflow at the lake. Many sat on the grass chugging from water bottles. The altar held votives, petit four cakes, fans, perfume, Catholic saints, jewelry, dolls, sequined flags, and bottles of rum, an assemblage installation worthy of a gallery. A troupe of drummers started their upbeat banging and clanging. Others chanted as Glassman drew patterns of veve, Vodou symbols, with cornmeal at the base of a statue depicting Laveau holding a gris-gris bag. Observers were invited to contribute offerings, and some came forward with fruit or flowers.

"Manjelwa" means to feed the gods, and each loa had favorite ritual dishes. In Afro-Brazilian Candomblé, which had the same roots as Louisiana Vodou, the warrior spirit Sàngó, or Xangô, loved a stew called amalá that was remarkably similar to carurú, the first recorded okra dish in the New World. Twelve okra pods were always stuck upright in the offering. Papa Legba, guardian of the crossroads, craved palm oil. Baron Samedi demanded rum. Beautiful Oshun wanted honey. According to Glassman, Marie Laveau loved elegant Creole foods, and fruits and vegetables prevalent in New Orleans. She also had a sweet tooth, which probably explained the cake.

The head washing began after sunset.

Glassman set bowls on the ground and grabbed handfuls of a white layer cake to thicken a soupy concoction of champagne, Florida water, and vetiver, also known as the oil of tranquility. Bystanders kneeled as she massaged the fizzy, sticky, weirdly fragrant brew through their hair, and then bound it all into a simple cotton tignon.

Only cake and champagne would do for a Vodou hairdo.

No seeds.

LADYFINGERS

Okra may do well in Hell, but it also grows in Arkansas.

Krishna Verma favored plaid flannel shirts, even on humid summer mornings in the Ozarks. She lived with her husband Jayesh Ramnani, a Walmart executive, in a bedroom community that was once a railroad stop outside Bentonville, Arkansas. Where apple orchards and strawberry farms once lined the road, now there were subdivisions fenced from view and occupied by Walmart home-office employees. Her chickens and ducks pecked around the front yard. A former IBM engineer, Verma had a real estate license and among dozens of other properties, owned a 30-acre lot she wanted to turn into a community garden as giveback to the diverse population changing the face of a region all too familiar with sundown towns, Ku Klux Klan rallies, and memorial statues erected by the United Daughters of the Confederacy. If that wasn't enough for one woman, she also operated a food truck called Indian Dhaba and sold vada pav to customers homesick for Mumbai street snacks.

Clutching a handful of okra, she cleared a place on a crowded counter in her kitchen.

"Atithi devo bhava," she said.

In Sanskrit, it meant "the guest is God."

...

The last time I heard someone utter this welcome phrase was in the northern Indian state of Rajasthan during the okra harvest in 2014, as a yellow dust storm blew in from the Thar Desert, and exhausted women field workers immersed themselves, saris and all, in tanks of well water to clean up after the day. Verma was raised in Mumbai but emigrated on an H1-B visa, met her husband through an online dating app, and settled in Arkansas, where in late July she prepped a catered dinner for a director of Crystal Bridges Museum of American Art, founded by Walmart heir Alice Walton.

"When I came to the US, everybody said, 'Oh, you are like *Slumdog Millionaire*!' And I'm, like, no."

"Is bhindi masala the same everywhere in India?" I asked.

"The only difference is the masala," she said. "Every region has a way of using spice. Like in Maharashtra, there's a lot of coriander powder in a normal gravy."

She sliced okra pods lengthwise with a paring knife.

"Okra has to be tender for me. If its gets rough, or spongy, I cannot use it."

Verma pulled out a bigger pod and handed it to me.

"If you press it, you can see the heart, the seeds are more developed. This one is going to be chewy when you eat it, rather than crunchy."

She opened a cabinet full of spices, and measured them into a bowl. Roasted cumin, coriander, garam masala, Kashmiri chili powder, cayenne. Salt went in, too.

"If you do an uneasy mixture, you will see the bitterness of the spice."

Verma heaped masala into each pod, and set the frying pan on the stove. The okra soaked up the spice as she stirred. She explained her style of cooking evoked the Punjab and Rajasthan, her family's ancestral home.

"This is what I make for my day-to-day life."

"Who taught you?" I asked.

"Mom! I'm happy that she did, otherwise I would have been dependent on somebody else for my food truck business. In India, it's such a strong patriarchal culture. And my mom was like, hey, the in-laws would blame us if we did not teach you how to cook."

Verma's food truck menu had fusion. Paneer naan tacos. Bhaji pizza bites. They're not really pizza or tacos, but she figured getting people to try something new would be easier if familiarized. A customer ordered curried chicken every day. She mentioned that food trucks thrived as Bentonville tried to keep pace with a rapidly globalizing palate. Fried chicken and mile-high pie were making way for dumplings, pani puri, bubble tea. Smaller groceries supplied fresh crushed sugarcane juice and halal meats. Bitter melon, loofah, and bamboo shoots sold next to purple hull beans and ears of corn at farm markets.

"What does the term 'Eve teasing' mean?" I asked.

"You saw it on our Instagram feed, didn't you?" Verma said. "It's what we call sexual harassment in India. Happens even here. This one customer wouldn't stop teasing one of my team. We scolded him. Next time, the cops."

The okra turned bronze, and the masala filled the kitchen with the scent of a desert caravan.

"They say that if you eat okra, you'll be good at maths."

"Really? Why?"

"I have no idea," she laughed. "Just people wanting their kids to eat."

LONGPOD

"Does it look like I deserve to be here?" asked Yer Lor, grinning.

She sat on a small stool pruning plants in the high tunnel at her son Ger's farm. She paused to wipe away sweat with a towel, and turned back to work, thin hair pasted to her scalp. Yer, eighty-three, was visiting from Minnesota to help with the harvest. She started gardening at age five in her homeland of Laos.

In the 1970s, Hmong hill clans that supported the American armed forces during the Secret War in Laos were given asylum status, and during several refugee resettlement waves, church groups sponsored families in the Upper Midwest, which had the largest Hmong population outside Southeast Asia. But it's cold up there for an indigenous minority accustomed to farming in a tropical climate. In 2002, members of the eighteen clans moved to Gentry, Arkansas.

The drowsy town had a Little Debbie snack cake plant, a feed store, a tattoo parlor named Two Guns, and a junction for the Kansas City Southern Railroad. The Trail of Tears crossed pastures nearby. A decade ago, Ger and Xeng Moua Lor bought a 40-acre farm set back on a gravel road lined with black walnut and sassafras. One side of their house was hung with prayer flags, and the Stars and Stripes hoisted on a pole next to the front porch steps. In the side yard, a grove of bamboo, a swing set for the grandchildren, a pear orchard. The garage had been converted to a cooler unit for cut flowers and produce headed for the weekly market stall called Sisters Sprouts, operated by their six daughters.

Wearing a broad straw hat and a windbreaker, Xeng dragged a wheeled five-gallon tub, jerry-rigged with a patio umbrella, into the okra patch in a field beyond the tunnel garden. The 58-year-old mother slipped on blue surgical gloves to protect her coral pink nails and reached around the waist-high stalks to snap off ripening pods, tossing them in the tub. The newly budded okra felt wooly like a caterpillar.

"It's a baby, and so that means easy to pick," Xeng said.

"If you don't wear long sleeves and you're trying to pick okra, you're going to be itching everywhere," said her second daughter, Pachee, standing with me in the field as Xeng went down the row. She explained Hmong women typically do the farming.

"My dad does a lot of the plowing and stuff, but he never goes to the market. It's always us girls."

She shaded her eyes against the sun.

"Hmong women always complain about how they want to marry an American farmer so then they can get them to do their work."

We walked through rows of eggplant and squash. A line of sunflowers cast welcome shade. The cicadas were louder than bomber jets.

"In Minnesota, my parents used to plant a garden for themselves," Pachee said. "When they came down here they saw the opportunity to own their own land. They love the Ozarks because it's so hilly, just like Thailand and Laos. They said this is like our homeland."

Two weeks before, at a Trump political rally in Greenville, North Carolina, a chant erupted targeting Somalia-born Minnesota congresswoman Ilhan Omar.

"Send her back, send her back, send her back."

The racist "go back to where you came from" refrain certainly wasn't new to Southerners. Taunts targeting people of color and immigrant communities had renewed agency, and in some cases were leading directly to violence, but just as often this xenophobia played out in subtler discrimination, like being charged higher interest on a business loan for your dream farm than the neighbor down the road.

"Like they're not directly saying it to us and not directly lashing out at us, but as a person of color you can definitely feel it," said Porlai, the Lors' youngest daughter, when I asked if the family had problems integrating after moving to Arkansas. "That's just how America is. We're all used to that."

The Lors worked hard to fit into their tight-knit rural community. They also knew other places less welcoming.

"But then we don't ever go there anyways," Porlai said.

They were too busy planting.

. . .

The US Department of Agriculture's Germplasm Resources Information Network listed 2,407 okra accessions gathered globally from Afghanistan to Zimbabwe. The plant material from Africa alone was staggering. India had even more. American seed savers conserved heirloom varieties like Grandma Edna's Cherokee Long Pod, Cajun Jewel, Choppee, Jambalaya, White Velvet, and Carmine Splendor. The Campbell soup company developed a variety known as Emerald in 1950. But most Southerners wound up eating the prolific Clemson Spineless, introduced in 1939. The Lors purchased their stock from a seed catalog company based in Minnesota.

Xeng headed back to the house to wait for a cooler hour to finish harvesting. Ger drove his mother on the tractor and his dogs followed behind. Shoes in piles on the front porch, and over the door, a wood carving of crossed swords, a Hmong shamanic ward against evil spirits. Inside, several grandchildren watched television while snacking on chilled watermelon from the field. Friday evenings were labor-intensive, as the family prepared for market the next day. Hauling in produce, boxing it up, trimming flowers, collecting bulk orders. Xeng's third daughter, Voua, told me her mother could make more money selling vegetables than her former work at a chicken processing plant. The Lors always had side jobs—house cleaning, wedding dress alterations, carpentry—extra earnings they could apply to a down payment.

Ger served as an Air Force mechanic in Udon Thani, on the northern Thailand border, right across from the capital Vientiane in the early 1970s. He showed me precious family photos, carried with them from Laos, hung in the dining alcove next to the kitchen: in formal uniform with a tiger silkscreened on his cravat, his training class graduation, posed in field khakis next to a T-38 bomber on a landing strip. He was 21 years old then. His mother Yer, showered and changed, took me down the hall and stood under a photo of herself as a young mother, with Ger on her knee. All fifteen of her children, including three she adopted, now lived in America.

One baby wanted more watermelon, so her mother, Tee, sliced pieces from a plate on the table. The little girl toddled back to the living room with a full bowl.

"We already know we're going to have granddaughters," Pachee said. "Our sons, they know they have no choice, they're gonna have girls and not boys, because this family's meant to have girls first."

The sisters beamed.

Xeng was diagnosed with Type 2 diabetes after giving birth to Porlai, who was studying to be a dietitian. She checked a monitor taped to her mother's arm. Dinner was usually a light meal after coming in from the fields, since Ger rose at four in the morning to feed their pullet chickens, and the women needed to set up their farm stand at the market in Fayetteville. Sticky rice, some vegetables, a yellow curry.

"Do Hmong eat okra?" I asked.

Pachee shrugged.

"Not really. We started growing it because there was a demand from our customers. But now Mom puts it in her egg drop soup."

KALALOU GOMBO

On the day after a mass shooting by a white nationalist at a Walmart in El Paso, Texas, I was still in Bentonville, and sought solace in the galleries at Crystal Bridges Museum of American Art. For the longest time I stood in front of an installation by artist Titus Kaphar, whose work rendered judgment on troubling moments in American history. His painting *The Cost of Removal* reimagined the portrait of Andrew Jackson, soldier, statesman, slaveholder, mounted on his horse Sam Patch, with his face muffled by shredded canvas strips hanging from rusty nails. The cloth was painted with Jackson's own words from a document estimating the relocation of the Cherokee Nation on the Trail of Tears. The embellishment, according to the artist, echoed nail-spiked nkondi, spiritually charged ritual objects invoked by Congolese conjurers searching out and punishing wrongdoing. The nails represented vows, signed treaties, to banish evil.

. . .

Wish I knew Addie's last name. She's long gone. So was my mother, who remembered the meals this cook made for a troubled girl sent away from home. Okra never sat well with me; it bloomed like cotton in my stomach. The slime made me nauseous, too. Even so, I ate a lot of it. Canapés of pickled okra rolled in deli ham, made by a church lady in Charleston. Okra roasted with nutritional yeast and hatch green chile salt by a preacher's son in Bentonville. Okra smeared on Creole cream cheese. Tempura-battered whole pods. Cornmeal fried chunks. Okra pilau. Okra soup. Okra fritters. Okra remoulade. Betty's gumbo. Krishna's bhindi masala. Xeng's pods, crunched raw in the field. Stewed okra and tomatoes, Lebanese-style bamieh, prepared by a former army cook who extended a dinner invitation while I was far from home. These tastes ranged from creamy to earthy.

But it took a conversation with Nigerian author Yemisí Aríbisálà to change my perspective, if not my palate. West Africans embraced okra's goo.

"It's a whole thing like a dance around this bowl," she said, as we ate breakfast in London, where she lived. "Everything has to have a bit of draw, or stretch, so when you pull up the soup with a spoon, it's elastic and doesn't break."

The look on my face made her smile.

"And okra is a first food. Easy for a baby to swallow. All that starch and glue. When you're brought up eating it, you don't question it. You just want these really dense things."

The mythic story of women arriving with seeds in their hair in no way softened the ugly reality that okra landed in the New World due to trade in human beings, and the feeding of them like so much livestock in order to get them to market. Amethyst Ganaway, a Gullah Geechee chef from North Charleston, said it best: "It wasn't something that was given. It wasn't something we had to learn to like."

These ancestors brought a gift we do not deserve.
Like a nkondi nail, okra binds us all.

—*Originally published October 2019*

Nominated, James Beard Foundation's
Feature Reporting Award, 2020

RAISING CANE

"Gimme some sugar," said my great-aunt Adele, who always grabbed me to her bosom and plastered red lipstick kisses on my head when I landed on her doorstep. She was kind to a shy, disheveled adolescent who lacked sweetness of other kinds in life. Like her sister, my Nana, Adele Anderson Rudder was the sort of Southern woman whose hair was never out of place, carried purses clutched with military precision on her arm, and marched staccato in matching heels, even on cobbled streets in Charleston's historic district. A descendant of French Huguenot refugees and Scottish traders, Adele was raised on Edisto in the early 1900s. Her father ran the country store next to the steamboat landing, where all the island's children bought penny candy. She could speak some Gullah, the unifying creole language of enslaved West Africans, but so did everyone back then, Black and white, even if they wouldn't acknowledge it because of race shaming or shameful racism. She taught me a little bit too, enough to appreciate its poetry and rhythm.

By the late 1920s, a swing bridge connected the mainland, and my aunt left to seek her way elsewhere. When Adele eventually returned as a widow to the Lowcountry, a certain condescending cousin, one of those Charleston snobs, reportedly said, "You moved away. What makes you think you can come back and fit into society again?"

Her reply, I'm told, was less than sweet.

SWEET SALT

A root word for sugar is śarkarā, meaning gravel or sand in Sanskrit. The related Arabic phrase was sukkar. From these, we got French sucre and Spanish azúcar, Igbo shuga, and Yoruba gaari. The accepted location of origin for *Saccharum officinarum*, possibly as early as 8000 BC, was Papua New Guinea, where indigenous people chewed on a wild plant long before its domestication. The spread of sugarcane followed migration routes westward across the Pacific Ocean, and spice trade routes eastward through the Indian subcontinent, the Middle East, and Africa. The earliest written reference appeared in a Hindu scripture known as the Atharvaveda, compiled around 1200 BC. Then it was called ikshu, meaning something desired because of its sweetness. Greek botanist and physician Pedanius Dioscorides included sugar in his *De Materia Medica*, circa 50-70 AD, the crucial pharmacopeia of plants used by cultures of antiquity. He wrote, "There is a kind of coalesced honey called sakcharon found in reeds in India and Eudaimon Arabia similar in consistency to salt and brittle enough to be broken between the teeth . . . It is good dissolved in water for the intestines and stomach, and taken as a drink to help a painful bladder and kidneys. Rubbed on, it disperses things which darken the pupils."

The Persians perfected sugar refining. Crusaders brought it home as a souvenir. Venetian merchants cornered the import market for molded sugar loaves and pyramids, some perfumed with violets or dyed with saffron; pastry chefs to Renaissance royals and popes created fantastical sugar sculptures known as subtleties. Bartolomeo Platina, the first librarian of the Biblioteca Apostolica Vaticana, wrote in *De Honesta Voluptate et Valetudine*: "There is no dish which cannot be improved with sugar." By the fifteenth century, large-scale production arrived in the Mediterranean, centered on the islands of Madeira, fueled by a craving for confectionery and the fortunes made from them.

And that is how we come to a sugar trader named Christopher Columbus.

Madeira was where Columbus married Felipa Perestrelo, the daughter of sugarcane grower Bartolomeu Perestrelo, the first governor of Porto Santo, and began conversing with Portuguese navigators about the discovery of the Volta do Mar, or prevailing trade winds, as well as the North Atlantic Gyre, a circular current that lured ships into the uncharted ocean beyond the western horizon. These atmospheric conditions speeded the Age of Discovery, and the centuries of exchange to follow. Columbus deliberately transported sugarcane seedlings on his second voyage in 1493. Within a decade, the first successful crop was harvested on the island of Hispaniola. Sugarcane rapidly transformed the economies and culture of the Caribbean, Brazil, and North America. It spawned the colonial-era molasses trade, an unquenchable thirst for rum, and, more dreadfully, the Middle Passage. Before the end of the eighteenth century, all of this would coalesce in the South, like the syrup dripping from hogsheads piled on the sugar levees of New Orleans.

. . .

Sugarcane and its derivatives became foundational for Southern culture. It's in the pecan pie and the gâteau de sirop and the corn pone. Poured on biscuits. Some fools—what the hell were they thinking—even put sugar in their grits. Women were expected to be sweet. So was the tea. William Faulkner praised drinking whiskey "cold as molasses" in *Light in August* and dissolved a teaspoon of sugar in rainwater from a cistern for his own toddy. Otherwise, he wrote, it "lies in a little intact swirl like sand at the bottom of the glass." A Southern-born conspiracy theorist named Robert Henry Winborne Welch Jr. invented Sugar Daddies and Sugar Babies. He also founded the John Birch Society. Fullback Bobby Grier first broke the collegiate football color barrier during the Southeastern

Conference's Sugar Bowl on January 2, 1956, when he took to the field for the University of Pittsburgh Panthers against Georgia Tech's Yellow Jackets. Ella Fitzgerald sang "Sugar Blues" in 1939; Bob Wills of The Texas Playboys wrote "Sugar Moon" in 1947. Billie Holiday once said: "You can be up to your boobies in white satin, with gardenias in your hair, and no sugarcane for miles, but you can still be working on a plantation."

Over three long days in 1969, the same year my great-aunt demanded filial kisses from me, The Rolling Stones holed up at Muscle Shoals Sound Studio, in Sheffield, Alabama, where they recorded "Brown Sugar." Those stark lyrics by Mick Jagger played on tight rotation as I snaked beside the Mississippi on River Road, heading west from New Orleans as the annual sugarcane harvest got underway.

MUSCOVADO

Patrick Frischhertz stepped over a drainage ditch at the edge of a field of sugarcane stubble on St. Louis Plantation. A tall man with auburn hair shaded by a Louisiana State University (LSU) AgCenter bill cap, the 37-year-old former criminal lawyer lit a burn canister and touched the flame to dry ground. White smoke billowed into the late autumn sky as fire advanced between plowed rows, roiling ash floating toward the Mississippi. Assistant manager Refugio Rodriguez Sandoval wielded a second torch, so the two brush fires could meet in the middle and cancel each other out.

The burning field smelled like scorched marshmallows.

"Some people still burn whole stalks," Frischhertz said. "They're farther up north where a couple of parishes have really low population density. We stopped that practice. Can't do that so close to town. Two years ago, I was watching a football game at LSU, and sugarcane embers were raining down in Tiger Stadium. I knew exactly who was burning that day."

Turkey buzzards landed, looking for leftovers.

"When you burn the residue, birds and everything else see the smoke, and they know it's dinnertime."

. . .

We climbed in his pickup truck and cracked open bottles of water. Even in late October, the temperature in Iberville Parish hovered in the mid-80s, complicated on some days by high humidity and an unhealthy air quality index. Clearing fields for the next planting cycle required the tracking of transport winds and a favorable forecast, made even more unpredictable during a hurricane season when the World Meteorological Organization ran out of proper names for the severe storms that slammed, one after another, into the Louisiana coast. Only the week before, Hurricane Delta roared past and punched down his cane, the stalks still warped in the aftermath.

"It could have been a lot worse," Frischhertz said, turning onto the dirt road leading back to the equipment barn. "Might have been steamrolled flat. And it will right itself. Cane takes a lot of abuse and keeps coming back."

. . .

Frischhertz married into sugarcane. His father-in-law, John Gay, was a seventh-generation planter. The family was intimately tied to the origins of the industry in Louisiana, and members included the first president of the sugar exchange in New Orleans, a founder of the Audubon Sugar Institute, a founder of the American Sugar Cane League, and even a King Sucrose, invested every year at the Louisiana Sugar Cane Festival in New Iberia. Yes, there was a crown and scepter.

"I don't claim the eighth," Frischhertz said. "But my son will be the ninth generation if he so chooses. And same thing with my daughter, although I have a feeling she's going to be running for president."

St. Louis Plantation was founded in 1807 by Joseph Erwin, only twelve years after Jean Étienne de Boré successfully produced the first granulated sugar in Louisiana, making it a hotter commodity for ambitious planters than cotton or indigo. A hand-drawn plat map of the property dated 1852 showed almost 1,000 acres under rotation: multiple fields of cane interspersed with corn, oats, and other cover crops. By then, the property had been taken over by a grandson-in-law, Edward J. Gay, a former grocer who built a white-columned house facing the Mississippi and continued to acquire holdings and interests in neighboring plantations until 1880. The Gay family papers, now housed in the Hill Memorial Library at LSU, were an important record of antebellum cane production, and the daily life of a sugar baron. Correspondence included descriptions of costume balls, smallpox and yellow fever outbreaks, political campaigns, the market prices of cotton, sugar, and molasses, and the construction of a railroad leading from cane fields to sugar mill. Many letters mentioned enslaved workers by name and documented their fate. A receipt dated February 1, 1853, for services involved in tracking a runaway slave named Israel, detailed the cost of advertising a reward for his capture, shackles, jail fees, and transportation. Also of note was a letter in 1860 from William Tecumseh Sherman, then superintendent of the Louisiana Seminary of Learning, informing Gay that a wayward relative was expelled from the school for smoking tobacco. Later that same year, Lavinia Gay wrote to her husband, worried what would happen if "old Lincoln" was elected.

Framed photographs of Gay's descendants and a red toy model Allis-Chalmers tractor sat on a fireplace mantel in the second-floor family offices, above the plantation's original general store, where Frischhertz paused briefly at his desk to read reports of quotas and sucrose levels from the mill that processed his cane. All told, he managed 4,800 acres of deep bottom cropland and timber, some still leased on a gentleman's handshake. He explained that St. Louis was also an expansion station that tested out new varieties of sugarcane, developed across the river at LSU or down the road at the US Department of Agriculture labs in Houma, Louisiana. The farm grew 17 different varieties. According to Frischhertz, all of them traced back to the West Indies.

"Breeding new varieties through traditional cross-pollination methods is the lifeblood of the industry."

Louisiana sat at the highest latitude for growing sugarcane, a tropical plant more suited to the climates of Brazil and the Caribbean.

"Cane is a returning crop, so we never have to plow the entire place."

"What time does your day start?" I asked.

"I'm up at 3:30 every morning. We're cutting roughly 1,100 tons or 20 to 33 acres a day, depending on stalk and fiber density. Sometimes means up to fifteen hours in the field to meet our daily tonnage quota."

"Breakfast?"

"A bowl of cereal. If the kids are up, I have whatever sugary kind they're eating. Frosted Mini-Wheats or Lucky Charms."

· · ·

Plaquemine, Louisiana, population 5,956, was named for the persimmon. On a hairpin bend of the Mississippi, the town was bounded by a Dow Chemical Company plant on one side, and the world's largest manufacturer of PVC resin on the other. A freight line rumbled through the historic district, where a *Confederate Heroes* statue erected in 1912 by the United Daughters of the Confederacy faced the courthouse. Following a reckoning on racial injustice in the wake of George Floyd's death, the city council unanimously passed a resolution in 2020 to remove it. Best Donuts was known for its hot boudin-jalapeno kolaches; the shrimp po'boy at Tom's Seafood came with a side of fried rice and egg rolls. The gas station doubled as a casino. At the junction of Louisiana Highway 1 and St. Louis Road sat the graves of Joseph Erwin, his wife, and daughter, dusted by container trucks hauling cut cane to the mill in nearby White Castle, Louisiana.

At sunrise the next day, a state-of-the-art CH570 John Deere track cane billet harvester busted through the canebrake, crop divider scrolls whirring like one of those battle mechas from a sci-fi film. The half-million-dollar machine had a striking resemblance to a giant praying mantis, whose mouth gobbled the crackling stalks, and then spat out chopped chunks through an elevator chute to be caught by an accompanying basket wagon. The wheels had been replaced with customized caterpillar tracks to churn through mud. In hours, this machine accomplished what hundreds of people once did with a cane knife. The driver smiled and waved before turning back into another row. A tune by Banda Sinaloense MS de Sergio Lizárraga could be heard through the open cab window. Dry chaff blown from the extractor drifted in the morning breeze.

Locals called this Plaquemine confetti.

The fresh stubble smelled surprisingly like cut grass. But then, for all its height and rind-hardened stalks, sugarcane was a type of grass.

. . .

Frischhertz pulled up next to my car.

"You want to go for a ride?" he asked, grinning.

"Oh yeah."

When the harvester returned, I climbed a ladder outside the cab, steel railings already blistering hot, and sat down next to Israel Huerta, a stocky 45-year-old wearing wraparound sunglasses. One of sixteen full-time workers employed by St. Louis during harvest season, Huerta, originally from Guanajuato, had worked on the farm for eighteen years. The Gays sponsored him for citizenship. He put the tractor in gear again, and we rode into the sea of grass. The cab was equipped with GPS, a camera for viewing under the base cutter, and a stereo system. Huerta told me he listened to norteño while harvesting. He leveled topper blades into position, and they sliced through the leaf sheaths.

"How long are you in the harvester?" I asked.

"We start at five o'clock in the morning, we finish around four o'clock. It takes about six minutes to fill up a wagon, about one and a half rows. But some rows have more cane than others."

"What will you have for lunch today?"

"My wife made me caldo de pollo."

"Are there any good Mexican places to eat in Plaquemine?"

Huerta shook his head.

"Not what we would call good."

• • •

After he mowed several more rows, I thanked Huerta, and jumped down to the ground, unwittingly stepping on a fire ant nest. It reminded me of a Swahili proverb: "The skin of yesterday's sugarcane is a harvest to an ant."

As I brushed them off my sneakers, Frischhertz explained ruefully that they had been introduced to Louisiana to combat the cane borer, but now wreaked havoc on bird populations that also inhabited the fields. He pulled out his phone and opened an electronic plat map created by the Department of Natural Resources. The color-coded program contained data on the cane planted in each field.

A hand-drawn map from 1852, updated for the digital age.

"What's beautiful about farming, it can be as high tech or as low tech as you want it to be," Frischhertz said. "It's just up to the farmer. We track everything down to the sub-tenth of an acre."

Even high-tech farmers must still battle brown rust, mosaic disease, cane borers, rats, wild hogs, snap frosts, and field-swallowing hurricanes. We pulled over next to a swampy canal to peer down at a petrified cypress stump. Frischhertz remarked that the topsoil in the River Parishes is ten feet deep in places.

A crop duster swooped low over a field being graded and reconfigured.

"When I first joined the farm, my father-in-law said, 'You have three big things to worry about for sugarcane farming. Number one is drainage. Number two is drainage. Number three is drainage. Because cane does not like wet feet.'"

. . .

Our last stop was the big house. The original was taken by the Mississippi in a flood, but the family reconstructed. St. Louis has all the classical elements comparable to the other grand houses built by sugar on River Road. Columned verandah, wide staircases, formal front parlors, a dining room designed for entertaining. Pantry and kitchen with a cast-iron stove leading to staff quarters at the back. I've stayed in many houses like this, some belonging to my own family, with all the conversations—or silences—accompanying ownership. Frischhertz guided me all the way up through an attic to the roof, and we stood on the cupola looking down over manicured gardens to the levee and river.

"How do you address the past of this place?" I asked.

Frischhertz nodded.

"As far as the burden of it, my wife Sarah and I have talked a lot. It's great that we can have these discussions now because they weren't happening not that long ago. I'm not just saying that to be positive. I'm doing something I love here on the farm, but at the same time, it does have a history of slavery. You have to be mindful and present to try to move society as a whole forward."

Frischhertz's in-laws formed a new company in 1983 with the immediate intent to change with the times. St. Louis Plantation became St. Louis Planting. Employees were paid a living wage.

"Everybody has a retirement plan. Everybody has a life insurance plan. Most everybody has some type of cell phone plan. We have radios, but it's a lot easier."

He voiced frustration about the green card process and the political roadblocks to citizenship for long-term H-2A workers wishing to change their seasonal residency to permanent status. The application for his assistant manager, Sandoval, had been in limbo for more than four years.

"I'm ready to pull my hair out," he said.

DEMERARA

Charles "Charlie" Schudmak had to shout over the roar of trucks that pulled through the mill yard hauling 50-ton loads at Cora Texas Manufacturing Company in White Castle, about ten miles downriver from the St. Louis fields. Frischhertz was one of 37 farmers contracted to send his harvest here.

"We call this grinding season," Schudmak said, as we crossed above carrier belts on a steel catwalk. "The cane deteriorates very quickly, so we have to process it within eighteen hours. We're dumping three trucks about every five to eight minutes right now." The 43-year-old chief operating officer wore a white hardhat and noise deafening earplugs.

"When you say deterioration, do you mean sugar content?" I asked.

"The sucrose in the cane starts to change molecularly, and so the complex sugars can't crystallize, or crystallize in strange shapes, and it reduces yield. Slows the process down too, because that stuff can get real gummy."

Schudmak was the fourth generation to manage his family's sugar mill, dated to 1817, when it belonged to a plantation of the same name. In a single day, Cora Texas had the capacity to grind over 19,000 tons of cane and produce five million pounds of raw sugar. The mill also processed byproducts like molasses for cattle feed and bagasse, the pulpy residue remaining after the extraction of cane juice, burned in separate boilers to generate power that kept the lights on and steam turbines running.

"We were green before green was cool," Schudmak laughed.

The catwalks were covered with cane sawdust and spider webs.

"Do you get a lot of bugs in here?" I asked.

"Only honeybees."

Cane moved into giant shredders—the stuff of my nightmares—and passed into diffusers, where the juice was extracted, then mixed with calcium hypochlorite to raise the pH and stabilize sucrose. Next, it went through a clarifier, and a series of evaporators to increase specific gravity, measured as degrees Brix (°Bx), until the juice crystallized.

. . .

In 1843, Norbert Rillieux, a free man of color born in New Orleans and educated in Paris, patented a triple-effect evaporator that revolutionized the technique of turning syrup into sugar. Not much about the process had changed in over 170 years, only the scale, and at Cora Texas, the crystallization vessels, called vacuum pans, were massive. I could see hot juice sloshing around through a porthole.

Schudmak explained that each pan of sugar boiled under pressure was called a strike: "Because they used to hit the pan with a hammer to break the vacuum." Seed crystals were suspended in this mother liquid, or massecuite, and a centrifuge drum separated the syrup into molasses and raw sugar. The Dutch word stroop (syrup) was the root for blackstrap, brown sugar was also known as Barbados or muscovado, and demerara was named for the sugar-growing region in Guyana. The British had Lyle's Golden Syrup. The South had Steen's Pure Cane Syrup. And, inevitably, we all had what my health-nut mother once referred to as White Death.

Before arriving at the mill, Frischhertz told me the art of making sugar happened at this stage: H-2B workers with an extremely specific skill set examined crystal samples under a magnifying glass, and instinctively knew when it's time to strike and pull the plug on the pans.

Most apprenticed for years. Technology, he claimed, had not caught up with this ability, and these artisans followed wherever the harvest took them, from the Dominican Republic to Brazil to Louisiana.

Schudmak hiked down a series of stairs to the mill floor. He stopped next to a conveyor and grabbed a red plastic scoop.

"Want to try some?"

The raw sugar was still hot, like sand in the Sahara.

Before being transported to a refinery farther south in Gramercy, Louisiana, the overflow was stored in two warehouses behind the main factory. These resembled airplane hangers. We ducked inside the smaller one.

My jaw dropped.

A mountain of sugar. An absolute pyramid, 77 feet high, 110 million pounds. It reminded me of artist Kara Walker's 2014 installation at the abandoned Domino Sugar Refinery in Brooklyn, New York, a hypersexual sphinx titled *A Subtlety, or the Marvelous Sugar Baby*. Her intent was to reference the subtleties designed for pampered royalty at the cost of those who labored in bondage. The mound in White Castle was less freighted, but still a testament to how our tastes continued to be refined by sugar.

"My kids climbed it," Schudmak said. "When they came back down, they were barefoot. I had to call the refinery to be on the lookout for lost sneakers."

TREACLE

Charles Poirier picked up stray shingles torn from the roof of a church next door to his house in Lafayette Parish. The cane patch growing in his backyard looked almost as tattered.

"You see how high it is?" he asked. "Well, yeah, that's probably, I don't know, six or seven feet. That cane ought to be about thirteen feet tall. Half is lying down and the tops turned up. It's a mangled mess."

"So was that Laura or Delta?" I asked.

"Both of them."

He climbed into the cane and pulled up some of the crooked stalks whammied by double hurricanes.

"And this is probably, I don't know, the sixth or seventh consecutive year, a little storm will come through, and usually right before it's time to harvest. I'm learning not to complain and just deal with it."

The latest storm knocked the bejesus out of Lake Charles, eighty miles west of his house in Youngsville, and more direct hits arrived soon after.

"See this right here? Big old purple cane. That makes some beautiful syrup."

Poirier pulled apart another batch to hunt for ribbon cane, distinguished by pretty bands of purple and green beneath the outer rind.

"The bad thing about these old varieties, the longer time goes, and you keep on replanting, they degenerate. Size decreases. Sucrose goes down."

The 47-year-old mechanic worked for the local municipality but devoted his spare time to collecting and refurbishing antique farm equipment. He also rescued an abandoned Goldens' Foundry & Machine Company No. 27 horizontal belt three-roller cane mill, patented in 1904 and manufactured in Columbus, Georgia. And that led to building a sugar shack behind the house where he grew up in Lafayette Parish, on the remaining land once farmed by his paternal grandfather, whose cane knife he used to chop down stalks by hand.

"What kind of idiot does that?" he said. "That's what some people say when they see me out there cutting with my cane knife. My grandpa was the last generation to farm sugarcane. He was a sharecropper, but was able to buy 100 acres in 1936, and paid it off in a little over two years. He left his cane equipment to my dad, who worked offshore, and still always grew a little bit, a 15-foot row, for us to chew as kids."

. . .

The next day, Poirier started boiling syrup before dawn in his sugar shack. He finished feeding one ton of cane through his mill and channeled 120 gallons of juice into a pair of custom-forged cast iron kettles. (Back in 2005, he cooked his first batch of cane syrup in a pork cracklings pot.) Poirier positioned propane burners underneath the round brick housing and fired them up. The weather had turned cool, a relief really, as boiling cane juice could be a steamy task.

"The higher the sucrose, the less I have to boil it."

South Louisiana was once populated with amateur backyard boilers. Cajuns took pride in making their own syrup. Poirier kept the tradition alive with immense finesse. He didn't exactly break for lunch—fried catfish and crawfish étouffée from a local takeout—but rather, balanced the clamshell in one hand, while with the other, skimmed scum and other impurities using a homemade fine-mesh sieve. It took all day to reduce and thicken the syrup, slowly turning honey-gold in hue, as antique Emerson electric fans whirred in the screen windows.

"Out of this batch, I'll probably get twenty-one gallons, which is actually good."

"When is the season over?" I asked.

"Not 'til we get our first killing freeze."

As the syrup got closer to its finishing point, Poirier dipped a precision hydrometer in the kettle to measure density.

"I'll usually bring it up to thirty-two, that's like maple. I'll go 33, 33 and a half, sometimes 34."

The soft-spoken mechanic handed me a spoon, and I blew on the hot syrup until it cooled a little. At 33 Brix, it still had a hint of grass; the next spoonful, at 34, the taste of molasses was more forward.

Poirier scooped the syrup out of the kettles and poured it in a 25-gallon Maxant bottling tank. After wheeling it to his workbench, the top was wrapped with cellophane and then covered in a blanket. He explained that the longer it stays warm, the darker the syrup becomes. A good measure of this first batch was reserved for chef Melissa Martin of Mosquito Supper Club in New Orleans. Her gâteau de sirop, a Cajun cane syrup coffee cake, was based on the one she remembered her mother baking on Bayou Petit Caillou, from a commercial "back of the can" recipe. Cakes were still a big part of afternoon coffee breaks in the bayou. Martin told me she remembered stopping by an old cane mill to buy syrup, ladled in a jar still hot, and gingerly placed on the floor of the car for the ride home.

After hosing down the kettles, Poirier carried the bucket of skimmed liquid outside, where the spent cane was piled on a trailer for removal.

"I was scratching like a cat what to do with the bagasse. Then I found a friend who raises Black Angus, and he takes it all. They love chewing on it."

. . .

Next to his sugar shack, old plow attachments were lined up, awaiting restoration.

"Want to see something super rare?" he asked, opening the door to his garage.

A rooster red 1954 International Harvester McCormick Farmall Super MTA-V High Clearance row-crop tractor was parked in one bay. A model designed expressly for small family operations like his grandfather's 100-acre farm.

"Only sixty-four were ever made," he tells me.

Poirier explained he would drive by places in the parish where they sat unused. The owners refused to sell at the time.

"A few years after, a friend of mine calls. He goes, 'Charles, may come pass by and tell me what you think I've got.' Well, I drove up to his house, and I saw the back end of this, you know, good trash. He got my dang tractor. So I said, 'Look, if ever you go to sell it, let me know. Make your price.' About twelve years later, he calls me, he goes, 'Man, come pay me a visit and talk about this thing.' And I said, 'If ever I would get it, I would pull out all the stops restoring it.' That was three years ago."

He patted the engine housing.

"There she is."

IKSHU

"Cornelia didn't want to talk to me at first," said Nik Heynen. "It took so long to build trust. And then she passed away."

A professor of geography at the University of Georgia, he pulled a mask over his salt-and-pepper beard before boarding the state-operated ferry to Sapelo Island, off the coast of Savannah. Tattoos on his arms, a trucker snapback, crisp black overalls, he looked more country rocker than academic. His concentration investigated the impact of humans on the Earth, and vice versa, but now and then, understanding these dynamics involved plain old digging in the dirt. Other passengers paid their $5, and we all waited on the top deck until the McIntosh County school bus dropped off three students heading home for the day.

For people from the mainland, crossing over the water would not have the same framework, but for those known as Sapelo descendants, riding through the Doboy Sound estuary out to this Georgia barrier island was a passage that may bring to mind earlier arrivals.

A woman who overheard our conversation begged us to stop talking politics. Who can blame her? Georgia, a few weeks earlier, was on everyone's mind. Mortified, I looked out across the spartina.

When we reached the landing pier, trucks and side-by-side mules waited for passengers. Walking past a pile of luggage belonging to a returning resident, I spotted dried plants with leaves turned silver and roots intact, and recognized it as life everlasting. Maurice Bailey, a heavily muscled man with wire-rim glasses and a Biden 2020 hat, tossed my bag in his pickup, decorated with bumper stickers that read "Save the Land" and "Proud Saltwater Geechee." We drove toward Hog Hammock. Rain started to fall. First drizzle, then heavier, and in another moment, typical of the squalls that blew in from the Atlantic, impossible to see through the windshield.

"It's dark soon, so we're getting right into it," he said, pulling over to a field shielded by saw palmetto and loblolly pine. He grabbed a Stihl brush cutter out of the back and walked into the patch of purple ribbon cane.

. . .

Sugarcane first came to Sapelo when Thomas Spalding, a tidewater planter, acquired the south end of this 16,500-acre barrier island in the early nineteenth century, and began to grow the crop commercially. He also built a sugar mill, with a cane press and curing house. By 1843, at the height of his tenure, he secured all but 600 acres of interior land. Upwards of 384 enslaved workers labored on Spalding's plantation. The most notable was Bilali Muhammad, born in Guinea, and sold into slavery as a young man. First transported to the Bahamas, he eventually arrived in Georgia some time after 1802 and was appointed head driver for Spalding's plantation. Literate in Arabic, and a practicing Muslim, his influence on the small Geechee community, current permanent population twenty-eight, was tribute to generational resilience. Pews in the Sapelo First African Baptist Church, founded by freedmen in 1866, were oriented to the east. His handwritten manuscript on sharia practices in West Africa was held in the Hargrett Rare Book and Manuscript Library at the University of Georgia. It was the first Islamic text written in America. Bilali died in 1857, and his burial site remained undisclosed.

Bailey was a direct descendant.

After the death of his mother, he had a calling to answer.

Cornelia Walker Bailey was a storyteller, historian, and griot. Her memoir, *God, Dr. Buzzard, and the Bolito Man: A Saltwater Geechee Talks About Life on Sapelo Island*, was an essential account of saltwater (island rather than mainland) folkways. She was also a standard-bearer for self-determination and a fierce advocate of several food sovereignty projects to propagate heritage crops—red peas and sour oranges and purple ribbon cane—once grown in the kitchen gardens here. What Heynen and her son, among so many other practitioners, called "liberation farming."

This year they planted three acres of sugarcane.

. . .

Hog Hammock was the last remaining Geechee community on Sapelo. The rest closed long ago. Tobacco tycoon R.J. Reynolds Jr., who forced descendants off their land so he could create a hunting preserve, had a lot of explaining to do to his god. Litigation over inheritance and land transfer fractured this population more. The island's highest elevation was seven feet above sea level, but Hog Hammock sat at a low point between hand-dug drainage canals and a stretch of maritime forest separating beach dunes on the Atlantic side. The Baptist church, grocery store, post office, and a library were the only public services. A sign on the unpaved road acknowledged Atlanta Falcons defensive end Allen Bailey was born here.

Surf boomed on the beach at dawn, within earshot of Bailey's backyard, still muddy after the downpour the night before. A stray cat weaved between the barbecue smoker and a white-painted school bus called The Spirit, parked at the edge of his property. Volunteers drank coffee on the porch until Heynen arrived in a truck belonging to the university. Work gloves gathered up, bug spray passed around, masks over noses, everyone climbed into the back.

"Are you going to take down the rest of the cane today?" I asked.

"Yes," Bailey replied.

"With just that one weed whacker?"

"Well, we got two."

The largest plot of cane was in a patch called Lot One. Several teenagers from Project South in Atlanta walked through the rows of white and purple varieties with branch loppers and topped the sheaths.

"We used the clippers to harvest for the first two years," Heynen said. "That was slow going."

Ayinde Summers, who created cultural awareness and service-learning programs for the nonprofit, started singing "Joy and Pain" by Frankie Beverly and Maze. Bailey chopped the stalks at their base, while others followed behind, gathering them by the armload. It was hot and awkward work. Mosquitoes swarmed. Tiny tree frogs croaked in the ditch. Fred Hay, island manager for the Georgia Department of Natural Resources, arrived with a small trailer. Within a couple of hours, the field was down and cleared.

"Sugarcane's not blocking out the sun no more," Summers said.

I grabbed a purple ribbon cane off the pile and cut a chunk with my pocket knife. I peeled back the rind and sucked on it.

No wonder.

. . .

Purple ribbon was the predominant crop cane in the South for most of the nineteenth century, supplanting earlier varieties, its juice higher in starch and plant sugar. But it nearly died out, surviving only in backyard patches, until Clemson University plant geneticist Stephen Kresovich collected descendant canes and back bred to a close approximation of the original strain using herbarium specimens as a template. On Sapelo, Dixie Crystals sugar arrived in the island grocery store by the 1960s, but it was an expensive treat for children raised next to canebrakes. During his childhood, Bailey recalled refined sugar was used sparingly, never in breakfast cereal, and added to sweet tea only on Sundays. Purple ribbon seedlings were returned to the island for planting in 2016, a year before Cornelia passed away.

Her son put down his weed cutter and wiped sweat from his face.

"How did that original batch go?" I asked.

"We bedded it up the first year that we got it," he said. "And by that, I mean we buried it in the ground, the old traditional way. When we dug it up in the spring, it already had shoots started. Then we planted those."

Hurricane Irma took out a large chunk of that. They replanted.

"In the old days were the rows narrower?"

"Yeah, but they were narrow because we did it by hand."

"Not at all like this year," I said.

He chuckled.

"Next spring, I'm hoping we'll have a tractor."

The crew broke for lunch, then returned to Bailey's house to stack the cane in a dumpster that would be barged across to the mainland for processing. Originally, Heynen and Bailey had hoped to boil on the island, but their kettle and furnace project was delayed by the pandemic.

They covered the cane with a tarp, and Heynen left to shower off mud from the field. Bailey cracked a soda and sat on the porch.

"Why are you cutting the cane and letting it sit?" I asked.

"It allows some of the water to naturally evaporate out. So when you cook, it's a shorter process. You're not spending all that time to get to the sugar content. Even if you wanted to replant, you'd let it rest for a week or so, before you actually put it back in the ground. That's what we always done."

At sundown, Summers built a bonfire in the yard, while his daughter and her friends huddled inside Bailey's house watching *Twilight* on television. Maryann Bailey arrived with a Lowcountry boil. We stood in the dark, cracking crabs. Someone cranked up the speakers. Then we sat around the fire, drinking clear liquor out of coffee mugs.

"Is Sapelo different from other Gullah and Geechee communities, like, say, on Daufuskie?" I asked.

"I must say a lot of our doings, we held on to because we were isolated a whole lot longer than other people were," Maurice Bailey said. "All we knew was each other, and how we do what we do to survive."

"When did you decide this was your calling?"

He looked up at the dark sky.

"You know, your ancestors appoint you to do this stuff," he said, his voice rising with emotion. "I was always taught you do your part in life. You got to do your part, and you won't have any regrets at the end of your life."

In her memoir, Cornelia Walker Bailey wrote, "Bilali is watching, he has to be watching . . . The spirits will watch over us and over the island through the dark night as we search for the first rays of light in the sky at dayclean."

The next morning, before leaving on the ferry, Maurice Bailey handed me a jar of Sapelo cane syrup. Rich brown, closer to molasses in hue. He explained that was the tradition.

"We want the original thick syrup. Not the syrup you get in the store now."

"But why did they make it thick?" I asked.

He smiled, the answer plainly obvious.

"For it to stick to your food."

WHITE DEATH

Whenever close by, I visit the great-aunts on Edisto. They're all buried in a row, sweet Adele between her sisters. I scrape off lichen from the headstones with a knife or wipe away tangles of Spanish moss that have fallen to the ground, then I commune for a bit in the shade under a live oak, its limbs furred with resurrection fern.

My part.

Unless you can claim lineage with the dead already at rest, this island cemetery is closed to newcomers. The church wanted to charge a shocking amount for a plot, so about a year ago, my brother Jamie scattered the last of our father's ashes in this row, and some of my sister Kaki, too. Belonging had a steep price at times. But it didn't stop you summoning the resilience of your ancestors, whether that means cutting cane in the mud and rain, or boiling syrup in a shack, or baking a cake like your mother once did.

I ate a candy bar, half-melted in the heat, all the sugar I had to give, and crumpled the wrapper in my pocket.

— Originally published November 2020

Author's Note: In January 2021, the Confederate Heroes *statue was removed from the Plaquemine City Hall grounds.*

THE
QUEEN
OF
DELICACIES

"Where the hell is this grave?"

Late on an afternoon when the heat index hovered near second-degree murder, I stood on a slope overlooking hundreds of squat white headstones descending row by regimented row to the railroad tracks at the verge of Rose Hill Cemetery in Macon, Georgia. Each marked by a dollar store battle flag stuck in the ground. A plaque erected by the Ladies Memorial Association identified the plot as Confederate Soldiers' Square.

I was clearly in the wrong place. No guitar hero here.

"Go ask someone," my husband Bronson shouted, answering his phone when I called home for guidance.

A man walking his pit bulls finally pointed the way, and I scrambled across a series of overgrown terraces, apologizing to the forgotten dead in an effort to find the man nicknamed Skydog, who adopted an empty glass Coricidin bottle as a slide for his Fender Stratocaster.

Established in 1840 as a final resting place and parkland for Macon's elite, Rose Hill contained a multitude of neoclassical mausoleums and obelisks, punctuated by specimen trees choked with climbing ivy, the ideal hideout for broke young musicians who wanted to get high on mushrooms and scribble song lyrics.

Helium balloons floated from the fence protecting their graves. Jasmine enveloped one corner where the first of the original band members lay at rest. A car pulled up on a pathway and several grizzled men climbed out. All lit up smokes and shambled to the brick terrace leading to the plot. They looked like bikers long past a last ride. One spotted me.

"Do you know where Elizabeth Reed is buried?" he asked.

I shrugged.

Another bent on creaky knees and scrabbled in the dirt, hunting for a rock to carry away as a memento. (Fans used to steal the decorative mushroom statuettes studding the graves until the family erected the fence.) After they drove away, I paid respect, texting pictures to my husband, the true believer, who should have been there with me.

The Allman Brothers Band formed during a volatile era of Vietnam War protests and the civil rights movement. The release of a live double album, *At Fillmore East*, including the song "In Memory of Elizabeth Reed," propelled them to fame in 1971. Before lead guitarist Duane Allman died at the age of twenty-four in a motorcycle crash, and was interred here later that same year, *Good Times Magazine* journalist Ellen Mandel interviewed him.

"How are you helping the revolution?" she asked.

Skydog's reply would become Southern rock legend.

"Every time I'm in Georgia I eat a peach for peace."

ELBERTA

Peaches arrived in Georgia by way of a circuitous route from China. The earliest fossilized peach pits, discovered in the southern province of Yunnan, date back 2.6 million years. The stone fruit known as táo was conveyed westward by Silk Road trade caravans, gaining its Latin name, *Prunus persica*, from a stopover in Persia—then arrived elsewhere as persik, pesca, pêssego, pêche—and finally, across the Atlantic sometime after

1539, when Hernando de Soto, who most likely carried pits among the seed stores onboard his vessels, landed in La Florida. Peaches proceeded along de Soto's trail from Tampa Bay to the Mississippi River. At least, this is one of the accepted narratives, since expedition chroniclers failed to mention peaches specifically. Another had peaches introduced by missionaries first to St. Augustine, and then St. Simons and Cumberland islands, later in the sixteenth century.

Once on the ground, peaches propagated so effectively that by the time naturalist John Lawson published *A New Voyage to Carolina* in 1709, he labeled them a pest: "We have a great many sorts of this Fruit, which all thrive to Admiration, Peach-Trees coming to Perfection (with us) as easily as the Weeds. A Peach falling to the Ground, brings a Peach-Tree that shall bear in three years, or sometimes sooner. Eating Peaches in our Orchards makes them come up so thick from the Kernel, that we are forced to take a great deal of Care to weed them out; otherwise they make our Land a Wilderness of Peach-Trees."

Lucky the pest tasted good. Peach butter, peach leather, peach cobbler, peach pie, peach sonker, peach marmalade, brandied peaches, pickled peaches, peach sherbet, peach cordial, peach bread, and an archaic fruit jelly called quiddany, all appeared in the earliest Southern journals, household diaries, and cookbooks. A recipe for ratafia dating from 1830 called for 1,000 peach kernels to be soaked in madeira wine. Lettice Bryan, author of *The Kentucky Housewife*, provided an elaborate method in 1839 for a jellied confection she called "A Dish of Peaches," the successor of quiddany, and precursor to those Jell-O molds laid out on picnic tables at family reunions.

Peaches were a rare sweet fruit available in abundance, even to enslaved people.

That's before they became an agricultural crop more valuable than cotton. In 1844, a London Horticultural Society botanist stumbled on the Chinese Cling growing in a walled orchard south of the city of Shanghai. Peaches were generally classified as freestone or clingstone, and fell into two further categories, depending on whether they had white or yellow flesh. From these traits came a world of varieties, but when the Chinese Cling, also known as Shanghai's Honey Nectar, was subsequently imported as a potted plant in 1850 by nurseryman Charles Downing, it quickly caught on in American pomology circles for its size and flavor, equally balanced between tart and sweet, with a distinct almond note.

Then the Civil War changed everything and nothing. Cotton faded a bit. Peaches flourished a bit more. Somebody still had to pick the crops.

From the Chinese Cling came the daughter peach we most often visualize neatly arranged in baskets at roadside stands or on the jacket of a Capricorn Records album dedicated to a deceased guitar hero. In 1875, Georgia peach grower Samuel H. Rumph crossed an open-pollinated Chinese Cling with Early Crawford, and the resulting juicy yellow freestone was characterized by a crimson blush on its cheek. He named it for his wife, Clara Elberta Moore. One of the earliest paintings in the splendid US Department of Agriculture Pomological Watercolor Collection is a Chinese Cling by Deborah Passmore Griscom from 1893. Her 1902 cross-section study of an Elberta affected by leaf curl sings of fruit gone bad. Yet Elberta became the commercial standard, so much so that Southern growers still identify the ripening season of other varieties either as days before, or days after, this prunus goes sploosh on the ground.

SCARLET PRINCE

Lawton Pearson yanked open the door to his silver pickup and a peach rolled out. More were scattered on the dashboard, piled in the center console cup holder, and tossed on the back seat, hues from sunny yellow to muddy magenta, in stages of decay and ferment. His office manager, Vicki Hollingsworth, called these "seat peaches." The fifth-generation farmer held a law degree from the University of Georgia but returned home fifteen years ago to manage the family business.

"One day, when I just came back, I asked my dad, 'What do you do for a living? What do you do? What do you actually do?'"

Pearson climbed behind the wheel.

"He told me, 'I ride and look at peaches.'"

Pearson adjusted his blue-and-white trucker hat over sweat-damp hair and rolled down the windows so the baked-cobbler smell in the hot cab swirled as we peeled out of the parking lot at the Pearson Farm packing shed.

In 1885, Moses Winlock "Lockie" Pearson and his wife Emma moved to Crawford County, Georgia, during the postwar era that could be loosely termed the Peach Rush. They switched from milling timber to growing fruit, but he died at forty-eight, leaving his widow with a dozen children. By 1917, their oldest, John W. "Papa John" Pearson, expanded the property with the purchase of a larger farm that included a boarding hotel for seasonal workers, a company store, a packing shed, and post office. At one point, he had 5,000 acres under cultivation. Pearson also patented a peach. According to his great-grandson, that didn't go as well.

"Papa John found an Early Hiley sport in 1946," Pearson said, turning down a dirt lane. "And an Early is always more in demand. You'd get better prices for them. He wouldn't share, so everybody was mad at him for patenting it. But then the market up North figured out that it was a miserable eating peach. The story goes he got a telegram that said, 'Have received your shipment of Pearson Hiley peaches. When will you send sugar?'"

"What happened?" I asked.

"If a peach ain't sweet, there's no point in it."

...

Pearson passed a row of crew houses opposite the old boarding hotel. Men done with picking for the day waved from the porches. Like other orchards in the South, H-2A visa holders from Latin America had replaced mostly Black sharecroppers, and at the height of the season, the farm employed seven crews, each consisting of sixteen pickers, two tractor drivers, and a crew boss; fathers and sons who had crossed the border for multiple generations. Harvesters walked from tree to tree, scanning fruit for color and size, gathering the best in a picking bucket strapped to their chests. Pearson currently had 45 varieties, and 50 others in experimental trials on 1,700 acres; the daily yield at the height of the season was almost 10,000 half-bushel boxes.

"There's yet to be a mechanized way to picking peaches," he said. "And it's going to be real difficult to teach a robot which one is ripe."

"When do you know which varieties are ready?" I asked.

"It's in my head. Have to be out there every day."

Pearson steered between rows of trees bowed with fruit, close enough so he could reach out and grab peaches as low limbs whipped the side of the truck. He yanked several, took bites, and discarded them. Handed me a couple as well. One had a distinctly boozy aftertaste.

"I'm always trying to root out the good tasting from the bad. I don't want to ship something that somebody gotta spit out."

Pearson cut another open with his pocket knife, grimaced, and pointed to a split pit caused by frost.

"Cold weather in March is what just makes or breaks us every year, so we're real particular about where we put orchards. Sometimes all I need is one degree. Just *one* degree. It's the difference between profitability and loss. If you think too hard about it, you'll go crazy."

He talked about altitude, airflow, and the equipment used to keep an orchard warm during a killing snap. Back in the day, hay bales were set ablaze. Now, wind turbines. Husbandry still relied to a certain extent on acute observations a peach farmer made among his trees every day.

"The birds will tell you where the sugar is," Pearson said. "Jays are mad for them. You'll see crows, too. A lot others you don't realize are here, like brown thrashers and mockingbirds. Although they don't like some varieties, they have preferences."

A pecan grove cast shade on one side of the orchard. The Pearsons started interplanting three generations ago, because a fall nut crop kept the lights on and bills paid after the twelve-week peach season ended.

"That's some really good peach dirt right there, but it will never get back in peaches."

"What makes good peach dirt?" I asked.

The sweet spot for growing peaches lies in a 20-mile swath of rolling hills known as the Fall Line, a geological transition zone between the Piedmont and Coastal Plain. Stretching from middle Georgia into upcountry South Carolina, this sandy, loamy soil essentially parallels what would have been beachfront in the Mesozoic Era. It runs straight through Peach County and is home to Georgia's "big four" peach growers: Pearson, Lane Southern Orchards, Dickey Farms, and Fitzgerald Fruit Farms.

Pearson parked next to his heirloom block, a grouping of tightly clustered trees less pruned than his commercial ones. Oddball trees, nearly obsolete, just for the heck of it.

"Most of these peaches we grew at one time or another, but they didn't have enough red color. Because now the consumer thinks red means ripe, and that's sad."

He pointed to each tree.

"This is Southland, one of the best eating peaches there is, and nobody grabs it. That's a Topaz. It often doesn't set well, goes all cattywumpus, still it's delicious. There's the Virginia series: Jefferson, Monroe, Washington, all the presidents. We also have a block of Elberta that can be traced back to the original tree."

"Hands down finest peach to eat?"

"Probably an August Prince or Scarlet Prince."

"Pie or cobbler?"

"Cobbler."

Both our seats were piled with fruit; a few more landed on the rubber floor mats. I reached out the passenger window and pried loose a desiccated peach wedged in the crotch of the rearview mirror.

"And this one?"

He beamed.

"Sun dried."

FLAVORICH

"I always think about young trees as small babies," Dario Chavez said. "When you first plant them in the field, you want to actually take care of them like a newborn."

Born to a family of dairy cattle farmers in the Ecuadorian Andes, Chavez first studied blueberries, then switched to stone fruit for his doctorate. Since 2014, he served as the peach specialist at the University of Georgia's Department of Horticulture, where he was offered his pick of land parcels to build a research station specifically devoted to nursing peaches. He chose Dempsey Farm, an overgrown 12-acre plot near the Griffin campus, an hour north of Peach County. Every major peach grower in Georgia had his cell number on speed dial; his phone kept jangling in the pocket of his cargo shorts as we hiked through the orchard on a sweltering morning.

"How many varieties are you growing?" I asked.

"About 185. All of these trees that you see here basically were grafted and propagated by us."

He bent to lift a limb loaded with fruit that was weighing down his new trials of dwarfing rootstock. Originally, all peaches had white flesh. Yellow was a genetic mutation.

"The flavor of a white is different, milder; it also has more florals," he said.

The Chavez Lab conducted experiments on pollen, germplasm, rootstocks, and the sugar content of peach juice.

The flesh of peaches could be classified as either melting, nonmelting, or stony hard. This meant some varieties had a firmer texture than others, more suitable for canning or cooking, while the mouthwatering "melters" were most anticipated when signs advertising ripened fruit appeared along the road during their all too fleeting midsummer season.

I began to melt a little as well. We found shade in a mixed-variety block, where the red soil was littered with brown pits from last season's fruit.

"If you want to grab some, you're welcome," Chavez said.

Several trees had white tape floating from their branches.

"We mark the plants that are ready for people to harvest. Anyone from UGA can just come pick. When we're doing research trials on yield, we actually gather all the fruit and truck it to campus. We don't send an email or anything, but people start telling everybody, and in an hour or two, the trucks are empty."

I reached up into a tree.

"Which is this variety?"

"Flavorich."

One of the pretty, freckled peaches came away wet in my hand. Then I heard plop-plop-plopping among the leaves.

"Oh my gosh, it's raining juice!"

Chavez laughed.

"That's the difference from getting one in the store, right?"

"So, pie or cobbler?" I asked.

"Ice cream. Okay, cobbler, because I can put peach ice cream on top. The growers sell it at their fruit stands. Cannot make a mistake buying a little of it."

Chavez walked ahead, happy to be among his babies. After standing too long under the obstinate sun, I sucked that Flavorich dry.

QUA-NA

"What's the difference between a peach and nectarine?" Jeff Hopkins asked. The farm manager at Clemson University's 240-acre Musser Fruit Research Center held up one of each.

"Fuzz?" I said.

"What else?"

Caught off guard, I squinted at other specimens arranged in cartons on a lab table.

"Uh, nothing?"

"Right. That was a trick question."

We were joined by pomologist Greg Reighard, who thumbed through his first edition of U. P. Hedrick's *The Peaches of New York* (1916) to show me illustration plates of nineteenth-century varieties favored by fanciers on the Eastern seaboard, including some cultivated in the Carolina Piedmont centuries earlier. Family Favorite, Late Crawford, Old Mixon Free, Summer Snow. Lemon Cling. Blood Cling. Before 1897, Blood Cling was also known as Indian Blood, Indian Redmeat, Indian Cling. An astringent peach with dark red flesh mostly good for fruit leather or pickling.

"Peaches were really a common fruit crop for Indigenous Americans from the 1600s onward," said Reighard, whose specialty was disease-resistant rootstock.

"Historically, this was a peach-growing area?" I asked.

"Well, it was for the Cherokee. But they didn't have the diseases we have now, and the climate had to be different, because they planted their orchards along the Seneca River. That's a low spot. We plant on a high spot."

The Musser orchards occupied Oconee Point on Lake Hartwell in Seneca, South Carolina, and lay above the Fall Line in the Piedmont region. The Upper Road of the Occaneechi Path passed through here; this Indigenous trade route network was a conduit for furs, shells, seeds, and other valuable commodities. Those peach pits, too, soon after de Soto marched to his vainglorious death on the banks of the Mississippi. The Muscogee Creek and Cherokee became the continent's first true peach orchardists. The Cherokee word for peach was ᎬᎧ or qua-na. Accounts by European explorers and botanists described villages along the great trading paths surrounded by fruit trees, which thrived until white settlers coveted those autonomous territories and treaties got trashed.

When President Andrew Jackson signed the Indian Removal Act into law, Cherokee leaders protested. On July 24, 1830, the *Cherokee Phoenix*, the tribal newspaper, published these words of Going Snake, a respected Speaker of Council, "Orders may arrive to prevent us from working in our fields, planting Orchards, or putting down wood to make our fires." Resistance proved futile. Land confiscated, livestock looted, farms and towns destroyed. Compensation paltry, if at all. Between 1830 and 1850, almost 100,000 Indigenous people in the Southeast were forced on a genocidal march across the Mississippi. The Cherokee named this deadly journey ᎤᏃᎯ ᎯᏓᎾᏠᎯᎸ, Nv-no-hi dv-na-tlo-hi-lv, or the Trail Where They Cried.

Their peaches went feral.

"No one was maintaining those orchards," David Anderson said, when I called him later for clarification. Based in Murphy, North Carolina, the tribal horticulturalist for the Eastern Band of Cherokee Indians sighed. "But this is where the nurserymen of the South came to get their genetic stock to work with, in northern Georgia, in western North Carolina.

"You find these peach trees scattered on Appalachian homesteads, freaks planted on tribal land for preserving and fresh eating, isolated in western North Carolina," he said.

Greg Reighard was fascinated with freaks of nature as well.

"When I started in the '80s, my predecessor collected a lot of what they call Tennessee Natural and Indian Cling peaches," he said, turning pages in his book to find the Blood Cling plate. "These were wild peaches growing in the forest or on fencerows. We also selected samples from some trees in the mountains two years ago. Someone told us about a pocket of them, but you don't find peaches as an invasive species anymore. Most times when I see wild peaches now is along roadways where people throw out a pit."

We talked about how different peaches got their names. Unlike heirloom apples, modern peach varieties lacked the same hype, although that wasn't always the case. In the late nineteenth century, the American Pomological Society had final approval of new name releases, and after the Civil War, the focus shifted from presidents and generals to hue and character, with an emphasis on sunshine and pretty ladies, hence the Belle of Georgia, introduced by Lewis A. Rumph, uncle to Samuel of Elberta fame.

"Hedrick wanted to stop these ridiculous multiple names that were coming up, like Stump the World," Reighard said. "He hated that name."

We left him in the lab, and on the way out to the orchards, Hopkins stopped at the walk-in cooler in the farm's post-harvest room. The potpourri scent inside reminded me of the perfume counters at the old Davison's Department Store on Peachtree in Atlanta.

"How are you testing for aroma?" I asked.

"With peaches, it's interesting," he said, examining bins of plums, apricots, and nectarines collected that morning. "Once you cool a peach, the aroma gets locked up. Fresh off the tree it's always going to smell like peach; if you get one out of a cooler, it takes a day or two on the counter to recondition and have that nice peachy aroma again."

Georgia put peaches on license plates and the tails side of quarters. South Carolina branded itself the "tastier peach state." The rivalry remained as deep as that between certain bulldogs and tigers. No contest, Carolina grew more. Both states were dwarfed by California, and China still produced the most by volume.

We walked across a sloping field into the advanced-selection block on the high point of a hill facing a sluice pond. Birds chattered in the still summertime air. Hopkins explained they evaluate hundreds of varieties for flavor and aroma.

"But these are ones that, you know, for one reason or another, may become the future of the Southeast."

He pulled several off a random tree, rubbed one on his Tigers shirt.

"One of my personal pleasures is to browse the variety trials when everything's tree ripe. I mean, just as ripe as they can get; perfect peaches. And they'll have flavors of coconut, pineapple, black pepper, lemons, limes."

Hopkins shook his head, wonderingly, and handed me one.

"How can there be so many flavors in a peach?" I asked.

We both took bites.

"Um, this is gorgeous," I said.

"Best lunch of the week. You're one of the select few that'll ever try this one."

"What's it called?"

He made note of a tag on the trunk.

"It's SC-10."

"Needs a better name than that," I said.

Later that afternoon, the scientist responsible for the SC-10 hybrid hopped on a golf cart handed down from Clemson's athletic program and drove out to the mother block. A Lowe's tool apron tied at her waist, Ksenija Gasic was Clemson's peach breeder and geneticist. She consulted her phone and counted down the row until we reached a couple of sorry-looking, buggy specimens. While commercial growers tend to keep heritage peaches as novelties, she hung onto them like an ancestral portrait in a treasured family album.

"These are the oldest tree varieties at Clemson?" I asked.

"Old Mixon Free and Late Crawford. I got the germplasm from the USDA *prunus* repository in California."

She walked down the row, checking for disease.

"I need to have a block where I can put the material that I like as the 'parents.' I can get pollen from anywhere around the world, but

I need a mother tree, you know, with the good qualities that I like."

Born in Serbia, Gasic emigrated to the States in 2001, and was hired by the university to kick-start a breeding program for peaches compatible with current Carolina growing conditions.

"Serbia has a different environment," she said. "The issues for peaches are different. That was a learning curve, because everything here is a month earlier, even the ripening times, you know?"

"How many trees have you planted at Clemson?" I asked.

"Around 30,000 over the years," she said. "Every year we would put in 4,000 trees, then in 2010, we put in 10,000. When they all started ripening, I said never again, because I would basically be eating peaches the whole week, and by the time I got to the end of a block, I had to start over again on Monday."

"I haven't had anything else today, and my stomach feels it," I said.

"The first week this year, I ate so much that my teeth acidified," she said. "Early peaches are not sweet, so I had to neutralize the pH in my mouth. A lingering taste on the palate can throw off the flavor of the next sample. But I couldn't stop, I just love them. That's insanity."

I mentioned the fantastic white peach. She brightened, climbed into the golf cart, and we went looking for it. We picked and picked, trying not to be greedy, two short women entangled among branches, arms stretched for really ripe ones inches beyond our reach. Pinky orange, the color of smudged rouge. Bins on the back seat of the cart filled with fruit.

"You cannot beat the white ones," Gasic said, "because the carotenoids that get spent creating yellow flesh, they all stay in the white ones and that's what gives them the aroma."

She took a breath, and coughed sharply.

"Too much fuzz in the air."

BELLE

"Oh! This cobbler is so good," Sydney Dorsey said, politely covering her mouth while juggling a plastic bowl, spoon, microphone, and the rhinestone tiara wobbling on her head.

Miss Georgia Peach had the first taste of the "World's Largest Peach Cobbler"—75 gallons of peaches, 70 pounds of butter, 150 pounds of sugar, 150 pounds of flour, 32 gallons of milk—baked in a brick oven lined with school bus floor panels next to the county courthouse during Fort Valley's annual peach festival. The line for free cobbler wrapped around concession stands and down the block.

It was a long day for Dorsey, from flipping breakfast pancakes to signing autographs at one of the orchards outside town. The 19-year-old pageant winner and her sister queens gathered early in the lobby of the Austin Theater, an opera house that had seen better days, where the five girls changed into semiformal dresses and reapplied makeup already melting. Dorsey wore a peach-orange pleated chiffon mini-dress and glitter ankle boots. The youngest, Tiny Miss Georgia Peach, was six years old. She had a loose front tooth, and proudly wiggled it for the others.

"Where did you leave your sash, Ava?" Dorsey asked, helping to bind her hair into angel wings.

Their mothers, one dad, and two pageant chaperones bundled the court off to parade vehicles parked on a side street. A field tractor with bins of fresh fruit. One Shriner, no go-kart. The deputy mayor in a flatbed. A lemonade van. A ladder truck. Convertibles for the girls. When the fireman burped his siren to signal the start, the peach queens rolled.

The Miss Georgia Peach pageant was revived in 1996—after a hiatus for lack of participation—and a talent segment was mandatory back then, even for the youngest titles. Now, the emphasis was on poise and charm. Scholarships, not swimsuits.

Contestants didn't wear hairpieces, cupcake gowns, or false teeth, known in the glitz trade as "flippers." For the pageant in 2021, pandemic masks were mandatory offstage, and the audience was limited to immediate family. The winners served as industry ambassadors during their yearlong reign while attending community events—the Georgia Peach Festival in Fort Valley, a Peaches & Politics rally, the District Eight GOP fish fry, even the Peach Blossom Cluster dog show. According to certified judge and board president Donna Long, the girls received invitations for all sorts of things related to peaches. The pageant was also a gateway to bigger competitions. Two peach queens went on to win the Miss Georgia title.

"How do you keep the tiaras on their heads?" I asked, sipping peach ice tea with the queens and their mothers at the Peach County Historical Society luncheon.

"See these clips?" Long said, holding one up. "We take pantyhose and thread it through holes in the base before we crown them. So when you put it on, the snap clips got something to attach to."

"Pie or cobbler?" I asked.

"Pound cake."

Having changed into "It's a Fuzzy Thing" festival logo T-shirts, the girls poked at their plates of chicken salad. Took selfies. Shared concession stand candy and kettle corn from the midway. Their mothers talked about the cost of pageants, hair and makeup artists. Tiara carrying cases. Favorite couture knockoff seamstresses and the brisk trade in secondhand evening gowns. Dorsey's mother, Tanisha, a former pageant queen herself, operated an online clothing boutique.

Is a fruit queen any different from head cheerleader or debutante? Maybe. Peaches and feminine beauty were conflated across cultures since the Taoist legend of Xiwangmu, Queen Mother of the West, who tended the Peaches of Immortality in her palace garden and decided which gods would be permitted a taste of the fruit that granted life everlasting. She hosted the chosen at an elaborate banquet known as the Feast of Peaches. Mystic peaches aside, what about the mundane kind baked into a giant soupy cobbler? Easily the subject of far too many sexy love songs.

Sydney Dorsey knew about body image. The reigning peach queen was awarded additional titles for prettiest dress, smile, hair, and eyes. But pretty girls could be bullied, and after her high school freshman year, Dorsey switched to homeschooling.

"There's not a lot of [body] positivity in my county," she said.

When you wear skintight gowns, ample curves could receive comments by judging panels. And they're not always kind. Stubbornly upbeat, she cited model and size-acceptance advocate Ashley Graham as inspiration.

"That's the thing about pageants, as my mom reminds me, it's just a set of opinions on a certain day."

The court returned to mingle on the midway. A little girl with hair tied in bunches stopped Dorsey at a lemonade stand and begged for a pose, face flushed with excitement to be close to a real queen. As Dorsey bent to give her a hug, the mother caught the moment on camera.

"What's your daughter's name?" I asked.

"Scarlett."

. . .

Several days later, at home in Swainsboro, two hours east of Fort Valley, Dorsey showed me her collection of tiaras. She had over one hundred, some mothballed in storage, the most ornate displayed in a converted gun case painted white and gold. In a hallway off the family room, she opened the glass door for a better look at the trophies, satin sashes, and rhinestone crowns.

"This is my shrine," she laughed.

"What is Miss Real Squeal?"

"A barbecue festival pageant."

Her path in pageants, Dorsey explained, started as a baby. She reigned as Teen Miss Southeast Georgia Soapbox Derby, Miss Uvalda Farm Festival Queen, UNM Georgia Teen, Miss Tattnall Shrine, Pinetree Festival Queen, Teen Miss Peach State. Her biggest win, Miss USA National Teen, came with a $140,000 prize package. This year was her second go-round as a peach queen; in 2018, she held the title of Teen Miss Georgia Peach.

"I'm a big festival girl," she said, straightening the sashes in the case. "And I love [organizers] Miss Donna and Miss Diane. They continue to follow your journey, whatever it may be. It's not like you give up your Miss Georgia Peach crown and you never hear from them again."

Dorsey learned hair and makeup with YouTube tutorials, and practiced on her pageant friends. In the fall, she was enrolling to study cosmetology at Southeastern Technical College, and then her mother planned to help set up a hair salon in town. Their boutique operated out of a spare bedroom in her parents' brick-and-clapboard ranch. Her gowns were temporarily hung between racks of casual wear they sold at pageant pop-ups.

"Red is my power color," she said, unzipping garment bags to fluff silk and chiffon dresses.

One had sheer side panels and a train.

"This is my baby. I wore it at Miss Georgia Peach."

A costume feather headdress hung on one of the racks.

"I don't know why this is in here, but I have Cherokee heritage," she said.

"You do?"

"On my mom's side. For one of my senior pictures, I wore this with a black bodysuit and jeans."

She tucked it away.

"You seem to have a clear vision of what all this can do."

"Yes, ma'am. But a lot of people think it's girls prancing in fancy dresses, and there's definitely a stigma around it."

"People make fun because you're in pageantry?"

"You can get on social media, especially TikTok, and they'll make fun of girls onstage or, you know, talking on the microphone, announcing who they are and where they're from."

"Well, that sounds like more bullying."

"My first year of college was completely paid for through the pageant scholarships I've earned. That alone should just make people zip it."

Dorsey walked into the kitchen, where her pet chiweenie, Ellie, demanded our attention. The peach queen flipped open an album and pulled out a childhood snapshot. A heart tiara tangled in her hair, she held a bouquet while perched next to a trophy.

"This is baby pageant me."

"How was that giant peach cobbler, honestly?" I asked.

"Well, my grandma makes the best cobbler," Dorsey said. "I know to go over to her house with a bucket of ice cream."

Before leaving, I opened my phone's music app.

"Have you ever heard of the Allman Brothers Band?"

She looked at me blankly.

"They produced an album called *Eat a Peach* in 1972."

Dorsey listened to the final track, Duane Allman's acoustic guitar duet "Little Martha," which he reportedly composed after a vivid dream about Jimi Hendrix teaching him the melody in a motel bathroom. The song's namesake, Martha Ellis, was a 12-year-old girl who died in 1836. It was also the nickname of his girlfriend Dixie Lee Meadows. Visitors still tucked flowers in the stone hands of little Martha's memorial statue at Rose Hill Cemetery.

"Almost sounds like something you would hear in a Lifetime movie," Dorsey said.

STUMP THE WORLD

"Did you eat a peach?" my husband asked.

"One or two."

"I meant in Macon."

Now would be a good time to admit that Bronson and I attended one of the farewell concerts at the Beacon Theatre in New York City, the Allman Brothers Band's favorite residency over its long touring career, just before Gregg came back home to rest beside his older sibling. The final encore on the set list that night in 2014 was a cover of Muddy Waters' "Trouble No More." A live recording of the song from the original Fillmore East sessions was included on *Eat a Peach*.

So here at the end, parked under a loblolly pine between the shrine to the Allmans and those Confederate graves, I scrambled for a seat peach of my own. Might have been from Pearson, or UGA, or Clemson, or any of the roadside stands in between; not really sure, because by then quite a few rolled around in the back of the car, escaping their paper bags after jolting from Seneca to Swainsboro. The peach juice dripped on my last clean shirt. Then the pit flew out the car window. Maybe a feral would grow in the peaceful confines of Rose Hill Cemetery.

Could someone please name a peach for Skydog? Until that happens, let's relish this passage from naturalist James Alexander Fulton, who wrote *Peach Culture* in 1870, a baseline textbook on the stone fruit that has come to define the often terrible but persistent beauty of the South: "It ripens in perfection only in the glow of a midsummer's sun; and the hotter the weather, the more delicious are its rich cooling juices. It is eminently suited to the season. When the weather is so hot that even eating is a labor, the peach is acceptable, for it melts in the mouth without exertion. It is the Queen of Delicacies."

That's a title worth a tiara.

— Originally published August 2021

Author's Note: In 2023, Sydney Dorsey was crowned Miss Vidalia Onion.

BLOOD,
SWEAT,
AND
TEARS

My father had a particular kink for used pantyhose. In the cool, dark basement of my parents' house in Newport, Rhode Island, he hung my mother's discarded Sheer Elegance nylons from hooks; inside were onion bulbs cocooned like an alien brood in a sci-fi grindhouse second feature. A fat knot separated each dormant orb, safeguarding them from decay.

"What do you think you're doing?" Dad asked when I hauled a bundle upstairs to the kitchen. "Put those back. Jesus H. Christ. Don't mess with my Vidalias."

Despite deep ties to the South, my parents spent most of their lives elsewhere. A homesickness for the landscape of their childhoods induced mail-order frenzies for ingredients from country stores and farms catering to Southern nostalgia. Liver pudding. Cow peas. Grits. A mustard-based brand of barbecue sauce shipped in gallon jugs.

Squat onions requiring creepy, loving care.

My mother never lost her Southern accent, or her love of humidity so cruel it could drown kittens. Dad was a yellow dog Democrat. They spent the 1960s in hippie art counterculture circles up North. Though they grappled with the systemic racism that defined their upbringing, they were not without shocking blind spots. And they never spoke of the most atrocious aspect of my family's heritage.

The memory of emerging from that basement with onions dangling in Mom's laddered stockings jolted me when news broke about a federal investigation in Georgia. Operation Blooming Onion peeled back layers of intractable abuse, including the variety that some would have us ignore or pretend doesn't exist anymore: the sale of 30 "guest workers" for $21,481.

Dark secrets lived on in the onion fields of southeast Georgia, where an unlikely crop with an outsize reputation had coalesced power and wealth not unlike King Cotton and Big Tobacco.

ROOTS

One of the earliest references to onions in a Southern cookbook is for oyster "soop" by Eliza Lucas Pinckney. Not long after, her daughter Harriott Pinckney Horry recorded a method for pickling onions. In 1832, *The Carolina Receipt Book* by "A Lady of Charleston"—believed to be Horry or her cousin Sarah Rutledge—included onions in a fascinatingly specific rice sauce, a Southern adaptation of bread sauce, which dated to medieval cooking in Britain. In 1839, Phineas Thornton gave detailed instructions for onion planting in *The Southern Gardener and Receipt Book*, and the process has remained largely unchanged. By the time Rutledge published *The Carolina Housewife* eight years later, onions seasoned all sorts of dishes, especially meat and game. Both the Union and Confederate armies consumed onions to prevent scurvy. Dr. Hunter Holmes McGuire, surgeon to General Thomas Jonathan "Stonewall" Jackson, apparently ate a whole raw onion before the Battle of Cedar Mountain in 1862.

Yet it would be another century before onions achieved cult status in the South, let alone a registered trademark.

In the spring of 1931, Moses Coleman reportedly made an accidental discovery after planting an overwintering crop of Crystal

Wax Bermuda onions in Toombs County, Georgia. They tasted sweet. Not candy apple sweet, but still lacking the pungency of *Allium cepa*, the species most likely introduced to the Caribbean by Columbus, and then mainland North America, when it arrived in the cargo hold of the *Mayflower*. (Coincidentally, the first experimental pair of nylon stockings was manufactured in 1937 and made its fashion debut two years later at the World's Fair in New York.)

While it is a cousin to the native *Allium tricoccum*, or wild ramp, most varieties of *Allium cepa* existed only because of cultivation and breeding. The one that would become best known as the Vidalia was Yellow Granex, a hybridized cross between the round Texas Early Grano 951C, and another parent, YB986, derived from a flat White Bermuda. In southeast Georgia, at the leading edge of the Atlantic coastal plain, the region's sandy soil was uniquely low in sulfur, which influenced onion flavor and odor. At the molecular level, it's also what makes you cry. The sweeter the onion, the fewer the tears.

Coleman managed to sell his crop of sweets for $3.50 per 50-pound bag, a high profit margin during the Depression.

He planted more. Then so did his neighbors.

A problem emerged almost immediately. Those juicy onions spoiled fast. Easily bruised by mechanized harvesting, they required intensive hand labor: tough young bodies able to tend crops in a range of weather conditions, on hands and knees, while lifting heavy loads all day long.

Vidalias should have remained a novelty sold at farm stands and county fairs. But New Deal legislation, starting with the Agricultural Adjustment Act of 1933, created an economic support system of crop subsidies and insurance. This encouraged truck farmers like Coleman to experiment. By 1963, Piggly Wiggly Southern Inc., which owned supermarket stores in central and south Georgia, built a produce distribution center in the town of Vidalia. That helped spread the bounty a bit farther.

Jimmy Carter shipped Vidalias to the White House and ate them with peanut butter on crackers.

Around the same time my father obsessed over his precious mail-order swag, growers were finally learning how to exploit their folksy roots. Or, to paraphrase Louisiana-born political consultant James Carville: It's the marketing, stupid.

In 1986, the Georgia Legislature passed the Vidalia Onion Act, awarding legal status to onions grown in a 20-county area. Three years later, growers petitioned the US Department of Agriculture to establish Marketing Order No. 955. (These orders regulated standards for commodities such as dairy, tobacco, and livestock.) The Vidalia was named Georgia's official state vegetable in 1990.

What began as a hobby crop on less than an acre evolved into a protected household name and an industrialized agribusiness. In 2022, sixty registered growers cultivated approximately 10,000 acres, with an estimated yield of 220 million pounds of onions valued at $150 million.

That's chump change compared with corn or soybeans, but still plenty to build McMansions on man-made lakes, sponsor country-and-western headliners at the annual harvest festival, and draw the attention of the criminal underworld.

More than onions stink when they're rotten.

TERMINAL BUD

"These are still cracking the dirt."

Aries Haygood, a stocky man with a closely trimmed black beard and shaved head, bent low over a row of top-heavy onions in a field outside Lyons, Georgia. "You see there, how the dirt's kind of separated from the onion? That means that it's still growing," he said. "The tops, believe it or not, have a good bit of life still in them, but it is time that these come up. We'll probably get in here and start digging on these today."

Haygood, juggling probabilities, decided when a field was ready. So many what-ifs. Rain in the forecast. A tractor breaking down. The next cycle of crops overcrowding nurseries. It's something of a race to the finish, after the Georgia Agriculture commissioner set the pack date. No onion sold before that date could be called a "Vidalia." He grabbed an onion by the neck, yanked it free, feathered sand off the roots with his fingers, and rubbed away the outer skin to examine the bulb.

"Right now, we're watching 'em every day, to have the size that's marketable. This one is about optimal for me. If every onion looks like that, I'll be in good shape."

"And appearance is really important, right?" I asked.

"Oh my gosh. Yes, ma'am. I mean, you know, we shop with our eyes."

As the weather turned hotter at the end of April, his six-week harvest was almost over. We walked along tire marks where a tractor had already turned over part of the field, exposing uprooted green onions to cure in the sun.

Haygood wasn't born to grow onions. After graduating from college, he sold insurance through the Toombs County branch of the Georgia Farm Bureau. His wife, Megan, on the other hand, was the daughter of an onion farmer. Haygood grew up in Vidalia; she was from the next town over. He liked to joke that she was the agent who brokered the deal with his father-in-law to hire him.

Of the 1,800 acres they owned or leased, 450 were planted in onions. Because the harvest season was so short, farmers couldn't profit from one crop. Haygood also grew watermelon and corn. His father-in-law, while semi-retired, looked after the family's pecans.

"I grow multiple crops to diversify, and lower my risk, to make sure that the bank's satisfied."

His first year as general manager of M&T Farms was a bumper crop. He joined the Vidalia Onion Committee, which administered the federal marketing order, and was soon named Grower of the Year. The farm's onions were sold in Kroger, Publix, Walmart, Harris Teeter, Wegmans, Sam's Club, and Costco. He custom packaged onions for charity fundraisers and sold direct to mail-order customers all over the country.

Haygood and a tech-savvy partner acquired the vidaliaonions. com domain name. A pretty good life, until he hit the bad year. Actually, a stretch of bad years. In 2017, Haygood found blood in his feces. That led to a Stage IIIB colon cancer diagnosis at age 34. (This advanced stage meant the 5-year survival rate was 50 percent unless the cancer was treated aggressively.) A year into recovery, his brother died unexpectedly. Then Haygood lost his father in 2020.

We piled into his black crew cab pickup and headed to another field. Jason Aldean crooned *You Make It Easy* on the radio. Gesturing with both hands, Haygood steered the wheel with his knee. Yawned deeply. His phone kept pinging urgent messages about tractors, seed salesmen, and the packing shed.

"Now I reference things to my dad's passing, my brother's passing," he said. "And it's like, dang, that was six months before I found out about my cancer."

"How did you get your name?" I asked.

He yawned again. Apologized.

"Well, my mom is Greek. My dad was all into Greek mythology at the time. So they named me Aries and they named my brother Achilles."

"It's spelled A-r-e-s, like the god of war?"

"Actually not. The hospital spelled it with an 'i.' My mom and dad didn't really pay attention until after the fact, and it cost money to get it changed."

Haygood drove past a weathered recruitment sign for the Sons of Confederate Veterans and pulled into a field of sun-dried onions where workers moved down the furrows. Most wore straw hats, dusty bandannas, kneepads. Each carried razor-sharp pruning shears to clip off tops and roots.

"This is pretty much the process," Haygood said. "And you see how much dryer the tops are, that golden hay color? Kind of looks like Rapunzel's hair."

He walked between rows, explaining the crop cycle. "The seed comes in little-bitty packets, and we plant high density, two million seeds per acre. It looks like turf grass. We grow those plants for sixty days, and when they get to the size of a pinky in girth, we start pulling the plants by hand and put them in bundles, 100 plants to a bundle. They're transplanted the first part of November, and usually harvest will begin about the middle part of April. "

I peered into one of the bulk container bins. Haygood told me it was filled with twenty fifty-pound bushels.

"How many a day can you pull out of a field?"

"Around 600 to 700 white bins. We've got around 100 guys this time of year, they make good ground, probably do 25 to 30 acres in a day."

. . .

Parked in the shade, an old Blue Bird school bus had a bilingual poster attached to its side. This listed OSHA job safety regulations, H-2A visa program employee rights, and the federal minimum wage. Next to it, a few workers paused for lunch, drinking Coke while sitting on upended field buckets.

Georgia ranked second behind Florida for the most H-2A visa workers in the country. Farm labor contractors and crew bosses were the registered middlemen who recruited, hired, housed, and transported migrant or seasonal agricultural workers. Think of them as modern overseers. Among other expenses, they're required to reimburse foreign workers for all visa-related costs in the first workweek.

Haygood's labor contractor, Nahum Ornelas, advertised on the Department of Labor's seasonal jobs website. The hourly pay was $11.99 for an onion worker. The piece rate was variable and usually based on units harvested. In the case of onions, that's a bucketful. For the next season, Haygood's contractor offered a $1.30 piece rate incentive to any who would pull and bundle the little onion sprouts. One competitor offered five cents less, another offered five cents more. Generation Farms, owned by a global agribusiness corporation, posted a piece rate for clipping onions at 40 cents per 25-pound bucket. That's not even rock bottom. One contractor allegedly paid 20 cents per bucket.

"They're always playing with me," said Haygood, mimicking his field hands waving a stack of bills. "They look at me and go, 'Big money. Me, big money.' And they're very satisfied."

. . .

That's how it was supposed to work.

But then, by 2015, and possibly earlier, unscrupulous contractors began cutting corners, falsifying applications, downright cheating workers out of their wages, and worse. The Department of Labor's Wages and Hours Division took notice. So did the Department of State, the FBI, the Postal Inspection Service, and Homeland Security Investigations.

When I asked about Operation Blooming Onion, Haygood expressed disgust for the charges described in the indictment. He seemed assured that his labor contractor was honest with the crew who worked his onion fields.

"It's like a family, a brotherhood kind of thing. We hate to see them leave. To think about someone taking advantage of those employees in a different setting? It hurts personally, because that's not how you treat people."

Haygood squinted in the glare as trucks loaded with onions headed to the packing shed.

"This thing means so much to me," he said. "I just can't afford for anything bad to happen."

Three years before, Haygood finalized transfer of ownership. The name changed from M&T to A&M Farms. (The old initials referred to his father-in-law and a partner, the new ones stood for Aries and Megan.) He had hopes for a farm stand and worried about an upcoming food safety audit.

He also found time to coach his daughters' softball team. Hunted deer. Seasoned onions with soy sauce. Hit his five-year cancer survival rate.

"I keep telling my wife that if anything ever happens to me, be patient and trust the employees to stick to our plans. We're still building. It's hard to see that value on paper."

We left the fields and passed through downtown Lyons, not much bigger than a whistlestop. On one side of the railroad tracks, Big Julio's Tienda y Taqueria, where field workers could wire money and buy lottery tickets, ramen, piñatas, and pointy-toe cowboy boots. A bus service stopped here for rides home to more than a dozen cities in Mexico. On the other side, in a wood-fired pizza joint, Haygood almost immediately bumped into the mayor of Vidalia hobnobbing with the chairman of the onion festival and a breeding specialist from Bayer, which sold seed and fertilizer to most farmers here.

After lunch, he took me to the packing shed, where onion skin drifted in the air thick as parade confetti. A plastic owl hung from a rafter to scare off nesting birds. Field bins were unloaded by forklift and stacked eight high to cure in a forced-air drying chamber. Women sorted out seconds as onions rolled down the packing line. Haygood walked into his controlled-atmosphere unit, where onions were preserved for extended periods.

Cool and dark. Intense funk.

These giant cooling rooms revolutionized produce storage, extending the shelf life and market availability of Vidalias for up to seven months. No more laying them on old newspapers under the crawl space or hanging them in pantyhose down in the cellar.

Haygood thrived on the storytelling that unfolded when he sold onions direct to customers at the shed. Folks would buy a 25-pound bag and share a cherished memory that revolved around eating onions at a table with their family.

"It's just intriguing to listen to 'em. It's so impacted them that they remembered a certain time in their life that they had a Vidalia onion. 'I remember we eat 'em like an apple. We eat 'em like this, I love to eat 'em on that.' I don't sit there and say, 'I got a certain ham at Thanksgiving,' you know?"

Most who stopped by the shed were older, in their 50s and up.

"As our state becomes a melting pot, we just gotta make sure that the tradition doesn't get washed away or overlooked," he said. "And I don't want it to affect us and us become only another onion."

APEX

The Blue Angels screamed overhead. Flying low in tight formation, the Boeing F/A-18 Super Hornets nearly kissed the town water tower. In pilot parlance, it's called a Diamond 360 maneuver. A real crowd pleaser.

Attendees of the annual Vidalia Onion Festival lay on the ground, sat in folding lawn chairs, cheered from pickup flatbeds, waved flags. The United States Navy Flight Demonstration Squadron does not perform just anywhere. Vidalia, population 10,847, was having its moment.

Concessionaires fried blooming onions in fairgrounds shaded by loblolly pine. A lever-action cutter flayed the bulbs, which were dredged in batter, and then dunked in hot oil to puff up like a flower. The Lions Club sold raw onions under an awning. A plushie onion mascot named Yumion worked the crowd. Onions were featured on T-shirts and tea towels, on cookies at the local doughnut shop, even on the city's police department cruisers. Farmers peddled their onion side hustle—relish, salad dressing, hot sauce, salsa, pickles, and cookbooks—at roadside stands. In the recipe contest at the community center, ladies entered pan-fried onion dip, onion pepper jelly dip, "crack chicken" dip, sweet potato tarts with caramelized onions, onion chicken spaghetti, baked Brie with raspberry onion sauce. The grandmother of Miss Teen Vidalia Onion won the $500 grand prize for her cabbage onion casserole.

The Vidalia Onion Museum had the smallest registered onion field at its front door, but the "Living Exhibit" was closer in size to a flowerpot than a field. If I was going to solve the mystery of onions and pantyhose, this was the most likely place. The attendant waved me into a room of memorabilia. Photographs of early growers, including Moses Coleman. Celebrity endorsements, newspaper clippings, old Piggly Wiggly weekly sales flyers, Miss Vidalia beauty pageant programs. An account of the 1985 onion war, when bootleggers sold out-of-state produce in Vidalia bags.

On the way out, I stopped at the counter.

"Have you ever heard about storing onions in stockings?" I asked.

The attendant shook her head no.

Some came to Vidalia for the Blue Angels. Others for the outdoor concert. And there were those who competed in the World Famous Onion Eating Contest. Aries Haygood's brother Achilles won when he was ten years old.

Don't believe anyone who says this is like eating an apple.

New Yorker Adam Zhang came down from Atlanta for the weekend. He brought a big cheering section.

"One more! One more!"

"Chew it, baby! Eat it!"

"Woooo!"

"Oh, he's going through 'em. Swallow it whole!"

"Oh my god. I think that one was painful."

Zhang smacked onions on his hip to soften them. His rival on the stage, Jonathan Flowers, bent low over the table, cramming each onion in his cheek. Flowers' training, he confessed afterward, involved a big breakfast and a Coke Zero. This was the second year they'd faced off. Both managed to gnaw down seven onions and split the prize money.

The little kids broke me.

An unwilling contestant in the children's competition wore a yellow gingham dress and bawled for her mother. Two boys with superhero face paint masks. Tiny Miss Vidalia Onion, whose green sparkle slippers matched her beauty pageant sash.

Most were barely tall enough for their chins to clear the table. Lions Club volunteers placed two small peeled onions in front of each. At the signal, Captain America munched valiantly. Onion juice ran down Batman's chin. Another child put his elbows on the table and held his head with a look of utter woe. The gingham girl, still wretched, turned away and clutched a judge. The onion princess wiped away tears with the back of her hand, spit chunks onto a paper towel.

The crowd roared louder.

"That's good stuff."

"Chew it up."

The father of Captain America grabbed him and rushed to the back of the stage so he could hurl.

The winner ate three.

TUNIC

Alma Young knocked on the door of a single-wide and took three giant steps backward. She wore black combat boots and a lumberjack plaid top, with a United Farm Workers (UFW) button pinned to her lapel. She carried a batch of bilingual pamphlets to distribute.

Most residents had left this trailer park at dawn, riding crew buses to the fields surrounding Tifton, Georgia, where the harvest had shifted to melons on a weekend in late July. A few remained at home, so she gave occupants the chance to peek outside before answering her greeting in Spanish. Set back from the road, the community was one of her regular stops. Young knocked on doors throughout the state, sharing information on the UFW's services and benefits: food assistance, COVID-19 vaccinations, face masks. Immigration and legal advice. Her official title with the union's foundation was Systemic Change Organizing Coordinator, but she served as someone who knew firsthand what it's like to live in a broken-down modular with a leaky roof and a fuzzy Buc-ee's beaver logo blanket shading the cracked windows.

Young was born in Matamoros, directly across the border from Brownsville, Texas. When she was eleven, her parents migrated before "things got really bad" in a city plagued since the 1930s by vicious crime factions—especially Cartel del Golfo—whose sources of revenue included drugs, prostitution, kidnapping, extortion, gun running, and human trafficking.

Her family wound up picking onions in Lyons, Georgia, where Young lived in her first trailer.

"Ours was tiny. We had separate beds, but there was never any privacy. We lived on the farm, so we didn't have to pay any rent. We also didn't pay for electricity or water."

She wore hand-me-downs from her older brothers.

On this day, the rising humidity kicked off an early chorus of cicadas. A rooster crowed and dogs barked behind fences as we walked around the trailer park. Rosebushes, flowering hibiscus, orange and peach trees surrounded some houses. Lawn mowers, bicycles, charcoal grills, a trampoline littered front yards.

Discarded bug spray cans on the ground, a shrine to the Florida Gators, angel garden ornaments. At one place, a toddler's jungle gym and tree house sat in a neat patch of cut grass.

"There's a woman living in that house," Young said. "You know what I mean? It looks well-kept."

Young mentioned that UFW started collecting donations of furniture when families described what was happening inside their homes.

"Beds, chairs, couches—they get ruined when it rains because there are holes in the roofs and none of this is getting fixed by the landlord."

According to Young, the standard monthly rent for a trailer was about $350, no matter how infested or tumbledown. Sometimes, the landlord was a former field hand who moved up the economic ladder, shifting from picking crops to better-paying jobs in nurseries, construction, or regional factories, like the custom trailer manufacturer in Ocilla. And some owners were labor contractors.

Back in 1984, the Georgia Department of Labor levied fines against several leading onion growers for housing infractions after discovering migrants living in converted chicken coops at labor camps in Tattnall and Toombs counties. David Okech, director of the Center on Human Trafficking Research & Outreach at the University of Georgia, called these "hidden populations."

In the spring of 2021, a dozen workers were allegedly discovered in a work camp surrounded by an electric fence. The Blooming Onion indictment noted that two escaped, hid in the woods, and were rescued by federal agents.

We walked past a mature agave, not commonly grown in this part of the country, and Young explained that it was planted as a welcome sign to indicate other migrants live there. Certainly friendlier than the homemade billboards in a field across the road, splashed with slogans in red paint: "Harris is a Hoe." "Biden Sez I Did It."

The United Farm Workers Foundation established a presence in southeast Georgia in February 2021. Formed originally as a union in 1962—most notably by Cesar Chavez and Dolores Huerta—the UFW protected the rights of agricultural workers, advocated for better wages, and protested inhumane conditions in the fields. It also focused on immigration reform, pesticide protections, and emergency aid programs.

Before she joined the regional office in 2020, Young finished her master's degree in education and worked as an administrator at Valdosta State University. She's come a long way from the onion fields of Lyons.

"At the time, the farmer only brought in H-2A workers to pick the onions, because that was the hardest work. We locals worked the little scallions, and as they got bigger, we would trim them. Once the season picked up, we would go into the packing shed and put the onions in bags."

Bland Farms, one of the largest onion operations in the state, listed extremely specific and special job requirements when advertising for 429 harvesters: "Workers will be expected to harvest, clip, bag, and/or load produce . . . . At no time will onions be dropped from a height greater than eight inches into buckets, or at any time during handling . . . . Workers should place the onions in the bucket carefully and with caution to avoid bruising or fingernail cuts."

Young was sixteen when she first worked the fields.

"And the last time?"

"I was twenty," Young said. "The reason why I left was because I was a victim of sexual assault, and I was afraid to go back."

Rape happened with appalling frequency in the fields and packing sheds. According to Human Rights Watch, female migrant farmworkers were particularly vulnerable to workplace violence and harassment because of the severe imbalance of power and victims' fear of being deported or losing their jobs. Perpetrators were rarely punished.

In southeast Georgia, one woman was allegedly kidnapped by her crew boss, held against her will, and repeatedly assaulted between September 14, 2018, and November 4, 2019. According to the Blooming Onion indictment, her captor also allegedly attempted to murder her.

While Young's job involved recruiting members and handing out household goods, her personal activism extended to protests on behalf of women at the Irwin County Detention Center. A nurse at the for-profit prison reported that female US Immigration and Customs Enforcement (ICE) detainees were sterilized without consent. A class-action lawsuit against the doctor who performed the surgeries alleged other medical malpractice that the women claim were forms of sexual assault. The jail lost its government contract and ICE detainees were transferred elsewhere.

Young always looked over her shoulder while in the field.

"I haven't had this experience yet, but some of my colleagues who work with immigrant communities at the big chicken packaging plants in the Atlanta area? They tell me that they've received death threats. There's a lot more at stake, as opposed to little tiny contractor, little tiny farm."

Sometimes, however, outreach was simply for fun.

"We do anything to connect with the children," she said, wiping her glasses. "One day, a church in Moultrie wanted to bring the attention to them by celebrating Día del Niño. It's a big thing in California, but not so much here in Georgia. So we did face painting for three hours straight."

The 39-year-old liked street punk and orzo with salmon.

Young dodged a large mud puddle in the unpaved lot. Noted a broken power meter outside an unoccupied trailer. Laughed at a sign over a boarded-up door: "Dolphins are so intelligent that within weeks of captivity, they can train people to stand at the edge of the pool and throw fish at them."

The dolphin is one of Cartel del Golfo's insignias.

SCAPE

The whistleblower ordered carne asada for lunch. He waxed nostalgic about his mother's caldo de mariscos. On the day we met in late July, two translators joined our conversation. He agreed to talk on condition of anonymity, as dangerous people wanted to know his identity.

He left Mexico almost two years before and hadn't held his youngest child since. Missed his daughter's quinceñera and his oldest son's graduation ceremony. Didn't get to kiss his mother goodbye before she died.

One of nine children, everything pinched growing up. Tight clothes, tight shoes. Carried a plastic bag from the supermarket instead of a backpack to school. Left at the age of twelve to work construction with his father. At thirty-five, he started the paperwork for an H-2A visa, and that first harvest season in 2020 was successful enough for him to want to come back again, but the second time, in 2021, he signed up with the wrong labor contractor and everything changed.

After our meal, we moved to a church, where the pastor gave us air-conditioned sanctuary. Waiting for the building to be unlocked, we traded song lists. He listened to a lot of norteño and cumbia.

"Do you like Vicente Fernández?" I asked. The beloved ranchera singer died in 2021 and a world of fans mourned.

He nodded. "El Rey."

We settled at a table in the church hall kitchen. The pastor offered us bottles of water.

"So what happened this last season that was different?" I asked.

The first time, the whistleblower explained, he covered the cost of a passport, and the fee for his H-2A visa was reimbursed when he arrived in the United States. The second time, a new contractor demanded money. A lot of money.

"At the time they contacted me, it was 38,000 pesos."

That should have been the first red flag.

On top of that, he said, he had to cover his own food, accommodation, and transportation without reimbursement. Another 6,000 pesos. All this violated H-2A regulations governing employer contractual obligations. He spent about $2,200 before he even stepped foot in a field. Nearly a year of minimum wage earnings—at $8.57 a day—in Mexico.

"I had to borrow to make that happen. There's a department store [in Mexico] with a BanCoppel branch where I could get a loan."

"Did you know what crops you would be working?"

"Not until I got to Monterrey."

The city of Monterrey in Mexico was a hub for processing seasonal workers headed to the States. Thousands a day applied for their visas at the American consulate and awaited transport north. He learned southeast Georgia would be his base.

"How was the housing?" I asked.

"It was a single-wide, four rooms, falling apart, holes everywhere. The room that I was in was okay, but the other rooms were infested with bedbugs. Ten people. They couldn't even sleep at night. If you got up to go to the bathroom, and turned on the light, there were cockroaches everywhere in the kitchen. Millions."

A typical day started at six a.m. The crew would prepare their lunch, then board a bus to the field. They'd work until midmorning, take a break, and then continue again for another eleven or twelve hours, sometimes in heat so brutal someone would collapse from exhaustion. Monday through Sunday. A half day off. The whistleblower explained that he got paid partly in cash, partly by check. His contract was for an hourly rate, but it kept changing, between $9 and $11.81. His piece rate was also arbitrary. Depending on the crop, the most he made was $138 a day.

"When you're working for a 'bucket per' contract, then you

have to move even faster because in order to make $35, you gotta have 100 buckets. So everybody's running at that point, everybody's running."

When the crew needed water, sought shelter in a downpour, or questioned paychecks, the contractor's employees turned abusive, he said, threatening to send them back to Mexico. To withhold pay.

"I have a contract," he told them. "I have rights and I know what they are."

And he discovered too late that the contractor added an open-ended clause in the contract—essentially the word "et cetera"—that meant he could be forced to pick any crop. He worked melons, peppers, tobacco, blueberries—and was taken to another state without his consent to pick baby cucumbers.

That's trafficking, as defined by the Department of Justice.

"Onions?" I asked.

"No onions."

It doesn't matter.

The whistleblower is a witness for Operation Blooming Onion. According to the Southern Poverty Law Center (SPLC), the contractor who allegedly extorted money from him was a known associate of a transnational criminal organization that the Department of Justice said was led by a 70-year-old matriarch from Nichols, Georgia, named Maria Leticia Patricio.

. . .

In the fall of 2021, as Vidalia onion farmers tucked their seedlings into winter beds, the United States Attorney's Office for the Southern District of Georgia unsealed a fifty-four-count indictment in *USA v. Patricio et al.* detailing felony charges for two dozen conspirators accused of mail fraud, international forced labor trafficking, money laundering, and witness tampering.

The exploitation of farmworkers and fraudulent misuse of the H-2A visa program were core to the charges. The indictment stated that over the past seven or more years the Patricio organization mailed false petitions seeking employment for over 71,000 foreign laborers and illegally profited over $200 million from the scheme.

The allegations were cruel. The victims were referred to by number:

#12 was kidnapped and raped.

#65 died of heat stroke while working in the fields.

#66 died cleaning a labor camp without air conditioning.

#42 through #50 were forced to live with a worker contagious with measles in a cramped, single-room trailer.

#15, #16, #17, #20, #21, #22, #23, #24, #25, #26, #27 and #63 were detained in a work camp surrounded by an electric fence.

#52, #53, and #54 were unlawfully charged fees, their documents confiscated, and forced to dig onions with their bare hands while threatened at gunpoint.

And about thirty workers were sold to a conspirator in Indiana for $21,481.

Kersha Cartwright, Director of Communications for the Georgia Department of Labor, confirmed that one of the indicted individuals formerly worked for the agency, and a second employee, Patricio's brother Jorge Gomez, recently retired from the same department. He was a state monitor advocate. Both were directly responsible for farmworker housing inspections. With regard to the allegation that Georgia labor officials were bribed by a criminal organization, Cartwright said the department had not been contacted by federal, state, or local authorities.

The whistleblower tried to move away, get a better job in a bigger city. Because he lacked a driver's license and his H-2A visa had expired, he ended up back in the same southeast Georgia farming community as those he said abused him in the first place.

"When did it get so bad?" I asked. "The housing, the work, the treatment of the contractor. When did it get so bad that you had to say something about it?"

"It was mostly the contractor. We're resilient to a fault, because of the living conditions in Mexico," he said. "I know I was being cheated, but what kept pushing me to keep going was the debt. Just having that hanging over my head."

Debt bondage was considered a contemporary form of slavery by the United Nations Human Rights Council.

"Are you still in debt?" I asked.

He explained that once he started working with a different contractor, he paid off the bank in two weeks. And he was waiting approval for a T visa, available to noncitizens assisting law enforcement in investigation or prosecution of human trafficking. (He had been granted Continued Presence and now had a work permit.)

"Do you ever bump into your former employers?" I asked. "Like in the supermarket? And are you worried that they might know that you're cooperating with Homeland Security Investigations?"

"No. I hope that because I'm here, others will speak up. Because what I'm saying is the truth, I don't feel like I have a reason to hide. But okay, sometimes we do watch when we go places, just to make sure."

At the end of the day, we trudged through a muddy field, emptied of melons he had picked the week before. A pack of coyotes howled joyfully at a fresh kill beyond the tree line. As thunderheads piled on the horizon, the light on grain silos turned silver.

If the whistleblower received a T visa, he hoped his family would join him, although his wife wasn't thrilled with the idea. He talked solemnly about his role as head of the household. He would like to give his children chances he never had, to leave them a legacy that would never be possible if he'd stayed home.

Aries Haygood, echoed.

These are his exact words in Spanish about the generational wealth called patrimonio:

"Hacer padre de familia," he said. "Prácticamente no, este, nunca pude nada, nunca un patrimonio para mi familia."

UMBEL

Wish I could quiz my father about where he learned to use nylons to store his onions. No one I asked knew, although some elderly ladies also recalled the practice. When I bought newly harvested onions at a roadside stand in Vidalia to take home, it did occur that the banded nylon mesh bag bore a striking resemblance to the fishnet stockings I wore as a teenager.

Kitchen folklore often got handed down, not written down. Dad liked a raw onion now and then. I don't remember him eating them whole, but my brother Jamie did. Nostalgia too often keeps company with faulty memory. While Mom and Dad avoided fully reckoning with the past in their lifetime, I did not have the same luxury, especially after a growing curiosity about my ancestry collided with digitized historical records and databases.

Some of my ancestors enslaved others.

Acknowledging the past was the first step, but there's more work to do. The broad rationalization that we should not be held accountable for the dark deeds of generations past does not take into consideration how closely so many descendants continued to live with that traumatic history.

For me, it's honestly easier to acknowledge my family's particular legacy now, since my parents are both long gone and their silence isn't just the awkward kind over the rice and gravy at reunions.

Everyone in southeast Georgia also seemed tight-lipped.

Farmers, contractors, seed salesmen, agricultural extension agents, even laborers. They bump into each other too often. At church. Restaurants and grocery stores and packing sheds. Barbecues and ballgames. Harvest festivals. Onion workers were afraid, Ulyssa Muñoz, South Georgia Lead Navigator with the Latino Community Fund, told me, and said they have been told to keep silent if they want to keep their jobs.

Several Operation Blooming Onion whistleblowers were represented by Victoria Mesa-Estrada, formerly the senior staff attorney on the Immigrant Justice Project at SPLC, including the man who shared his story and norteño tunes with me. She was disappointed that the federal investigation had not indicted more farmers. (Mesa-Estrada transitioned to private practice in August, but SPLC was continuing its representation of the whistleblowers.)

The term she used repeatedly when we talked about the case was "willful ignorance."

"Many farmers practice this," she told me. "'If I don't see it, I don't care.' They hire labor contractors, indirectly knowing it's shady. That's the sad part. A lot of farmers know, but they ignore the situation and wash their hands."

* * *

Only one southeast Georgia farmer was named as a defendant in the indictment. Charles Michael King ran Kings Berry Farm and was a registered agent of a packing shed owned by another defendant. Among the counts of worker exploitation, he was cited as aiding and abetting a conspirator who allegedly kidnapped and attempted to kill one victim. A job description for his farm on the Department of Labor's seasonal job website mentioned harvesting berries, grapes, and onions.

"When they do direct hiring, when the housing is good, when there's a compliance officer, a bilingual person in the office, things work well," Mesa-Estrada said. "It's an economic decision to their business, but they know when they're not directly involved, things go bad."

Sometimes, as Aries Haygood feared, you can do everything right, and things go bad anyway. After I visited his farm, he had to recall onions potentially tainted with *Listeria monocytogenes* after the bacteria was detected on his pack line.

Maria Leticia Patricio was still listed as the registered agent of multiple active harvest companies. And she remained on Spanish-language contractor websites, which continued to recruit new workers from Mexico and beyond.

A representative with the Department of Justice confirmed Operation Blooming Onion was ongoing and widening in scope.

Could the onion fields of southeast Georgia be the place of reckoning for the silences of today? I worry that it won't. While slavery has been abolished, it hasn't ended. Some people still treated human beings as property. Too many still profited from it. Southerners, especially, have no excuses for allowing this evil to persist. When Edward R. Murrow interviewed farmers for his *Harvest of Shame* documentary on migrant workers, one told the CBS reporter, "We used to own our slaves. Now we just rent them." In the same documentary, a minister said, "Someone else makes thousands of dollars out of his sweat. Is that a slave or not?" That was in 1960. And also now.

All for an onion that doesn't make you cry.

—Originally published October 2022

Author's Note: On July 31, 2024, the US District Court for the Southern District of Georgia Waycross Division accepted a plea agreement in Case Number 5:21-CR-009-1. Maria Leticia Patricio withdrew her plea of not guilty and changed it to guilty on one count of conspiracy to attempt mail fraud in the indictment, and agreed the object of this conspiracy was to make money from fraudulent visa applications, exploiting workers through forced labor, and hiding proceeds through money laundering. Her agreement with the court includes a recommended prison sentence, restitution, forfeiture of assets, and a temporary debarment from participating in the US Department of Labor's H-2A visa program.

The whistleblower has been granted a T visa.

THE
WOUNDED
FRUIT

"Watch out," I said. "You're way too close."

My youngest sister's index finger hovered within an inch of the 200-year-old oil painting.

"Hilary! Seriously, don't point!"

We grew up stretching canvases and cleaning sable brushes in our father's studio, so we were dangerously comfortable touching important works of art, but the curators at Harvard's Fogg Museum would have preferred that we kept a respectful distance. At that moment, no security guard lurked in the third-floor atrium, and the two of us shared a pair of cheaters to examine airy brushstrokes limning flesh as ripe and luscious as the red-hot lipstick worn by my first Barbie doll.

The perspective was amateurishly askew, the composition primitive, especially compared to ostentatious banquets once tabled by Dutch Baroque masters. Yet not bad for a twenty-something apprentice starting out in Baltimore, Maryland. I opened a website on my phone and zoomed in to compare a starker still life, also painted in 1822 by the same early American artist, that sold at Christie's for $277,200. The auctioned version was boldly centered on a blue-rimmed plate, with a juicy chunk fallen to the side, devoid of the dainty peaches and curling grape leaves obscuring the more conventional rendition facing us in the Fogg. Yet both represented a visionary expression of joy for the fruit that only decades later would become a tool of systemic racism.

Until artists across the South eventually created their own celebratory interpretations, seeking to reclaim power and ownership over one of our greatest visual feasts.

"See that?" Hilary said, waving her hand at blobs of paint. "Look how she used those tiny white dots to highlight the seeds."

A single seed clung to the pale green rind, slipping wetly from the exposed heart of Sarah Miriam Peale's broken watermelon.

MOON AND STARS

Much like me and my siblings, Sarah Miriam Peale was born into a multigenerational family of white artists. While most of the Peales churned out portraits of prominent socialites, politicians, and Revolutionary War heroes, Peale's cousin Raphaelle was the first notable American to focus on still life when it was snobbishly dismissed as a subject for amateurs. In her teens, Peale, affectionately known as Sally, apprenticed with her father, James, in Philadelphia, mixing his paints and adding her own brushstrokes to lace, flowers, and other portraiture details. She then shared studio space on the third floor of another cousin's museum and gallery in Baltimore. In a letter posted on December 16, 1819, Rembrandt Peale reported her progress: " . . . you will be surprised to see how much Sally is improving. Consequently she will become more industrious and I think it is very probable that she will find employment in Baltemore [sic]." In an era when women of a certain social standing were morally suspect if they worked for their livelihood, Peale became the first truly successful female commercial artist in America.

She also never married.

One of her cousins once commented: "Sally is as usual breaking all the beaus hearts & won't have any of them." Beyond that suggestion of an independent spirit, few original details exist about her personal life, as none of her own correspondence has survived, although a self-portrait at age eighteen highlights violet-blue eyes and dark curls, with rosy cheeks matching her crimson velvet shawl. Three years after her melons, Peale's father painted a similar study, with grapes scattered like marbles and a peach sliced in half, framing a less appetizing gourd. Not quite a copycat, but perhaps a wink-wink for his protégé.

In 1847, Peale left her family behind and set up a portrait studio in St. Louis, Missouri, a boomtown that solidified its status as a "Gateway to the West" when gold was discovered in California. During the Civil War, when the state seesawed its loyalty between Union and Confederate camps, Peale took up still life painting again. In 1878, however, she returned to Philadelphia to reunite with three other sisters, artists in their own right.

What would she think about her painting selling for a personal record price almost 150 years after her death? Not her dainty baskets of raspberries, bowls of ripe cherries, glossy bunches of grapes, peaches rolling, scattered on a table.

A big-ass chunk of watermelon.

"It really could own a wall," said Caroline Seabolt, a specialist in American art and head of sale for the Christie's auction that included Peale's work. When we spoke about the significance of the painting, she emphasized that while Peale was so young in 1822, her singular aesthetic and voice were already evident, even within a dynasty of talented painters. "It literally has a juicy quality, in the vibrant colors of the melon."

Then she added something that gave me pause for thought about the Peale fascination with fruit, not as a side hustle to their portraiture work but the breakthrough for an emerging American genre. The still life at the Fogg, with its addition of peaches and grape leaves, "is a formal study of the way natural objects interact with one another," Seabolt said. "But the one we just sold? You're looking at a singular portrait."

DREAM DEW

The watermelon, *Citrullus lanatus*, is among the domesticated fruits whose place of origin remains a mystery. Archaeobotanists speculate that a sweet relative grown in the Kordofan and Darfur regions of Sudan may be its progenitor. Other ancient varieties had bitter pulp, closer in taste to their cucumber cousins, and would never be destined for a Bucee's frozen slushie or my Nana's watermelon rind pickle. A quencher of thirst, the fruit is 92 percent water by weight, and for those toiling in the drought-plagued, semi-arid Sahel, often a lifesaver. The oldest remains yet discovered, from a 6,000-year-old wild watermelon, were found at a neolithic settlement known as Uan Muhuggiag in southwestern Libya. The seeds were cracked by human teeth.

But for art's sake, it would be best to begin with the timeworn relief of a green-striped melon, painted about 2,000 years later by an unknown craftsman on the limestone walls of a pharaoh's tomb in Saqqara, Egypt. It looked remarkably like the Georgia Rattlesnakes piled in the back of pickups at the State Farmers Market in Cordele, Georgia, self-styled watermelon capital of the world.

The journey, from there to here, across eons and oceans, was fraught.

Melon seeds crossed in the cargo holds of ships navigated by early Spanish and Portuguese explorers. Hidden in the hair of enslaved women, victims of the Columbian Exchange. Disseminated by missionaries and colonizers seeking fabled lost cities, silver mines, or simply conquest. By 1576, Santa Elena, the first capital of La Florida, was reported as fertile ground for watermelons. Carried overland on the vast network of Indigenous trade paths stretching west, adopted by tribes in the Mississippi Valley, the La Junta region on the borders of present-day Texas and Mexico, and Pueblo communities of the Four Corners.

Similar to its role in arid Africa, watermelon became a source of hydration in a harsh desert climate on the high mesas. For thousands of years, the Hopi practiced dry farming there, relying on rainfall and spring water to grow the Three Sisters—corn, beans, and squash—in the ceremonial calendar tied to Katsina, the Hopi religion, and when watermelon joined them, it was mentioned in prayers for rain during the planting season.

Hopi performers, known as paiyakyamu, performed ceremonial, communal dances to invoke favorable weather. They represented guardian spirits, expressly rainmakers. Between solemn ceremonial acts, they provided comic relief, committing acts of gluttony. Modern Indigenous artists depicted these sacred clowns gobbling watermelons. A paunchy paiyakyamu in mid-dance and surrounded by Hopi sikyatko melons was featured in a watercolor by Julian Martinez of Po-Woh-Geh-Owingeh (San Ildefonso Pueblo) in the National Museum of the American Indian. Or maybe he's sleepwalking in a dream state. In more graphic work, Hopi artist Rod Phillips showed Koshare, another name for this jester, clutching a hunting blade and melon under one arm while spitting seeds from a slice. Juice ran down his chin.

GENTILITY

On a day when The Metropolitan Museum of Art was closed to the public, Sylvia Yount, Curator in Charge of the American Wing, walked me through to Gallery 762. This small room at the back of the museum—labeled Civil War and Reconstruction Eras and Legacies—was an assemblage of paintings and sculptures that created a visual timeline and emotional sounding board for one of our country's thorniest turning points. A messianic portrait of abolitionist John Brown occupied an entire wall. A triptych of Black military service painted in 1865 and 1866 by Thomas Waterman Wood. The Augustus Saint-Gaudens bronze of Lincoln, standing with his head bowed. Union army veteran Theodor Kaufmann's poignant *On to Liberty*.

But I was here to see the Charles Ethan Porter.

He never gave it a title, and yet this canvas, painted around 1890, was known in the art world as *Cracked Watermelon*. Instead of a rigidly formal study like the trompe l'œil favored by earlier still life artists, this melon looks like it bounced off the back of a delivery wagon and smashed on the road.

"It is very visceral," Yount said, as we peered at the mushy flesh, fading crisp red to slimy white from exposure and rot. "Probably his most ambitious still life by this point."

Porter was among the nineteenth century Black artists—Edmonia Lewis, Henry Ossawa Tanner, May Howard Jackson, Edward Mitchell Bannister—breaking white art establishment boundaries, but unlike the others, he chose to concentrate on still life.

He became one of the first Black artists admitted to the National Academy of Design in 1869, then sailed to Paris and enrolled in L'École des Arts Décoratifs. Author Samuel Clemens (better known as Mark Twain) was a patron, and wrote letters of introduction to assist his study overseas. When Porter returned to America, he developed a following and gained respect from contemporaries like landscape artist Frederic Edwin Church. His most productive period spanned the 1880s and '90s; he painted a lot of pretty apples and roses. And two radical watermelons.

"This was kind of his golden moment," Yount said.

Despite this modest success, Porter's work fell out of vogue by the turn of the century. Art historians blamed rampant racism. More dramatic genres superseded gauzy Impressionism, and buyers became bored with Americans. At the end of his career, Charles Ethan Porter was compelled to trade paintings for food and board. He died destitute in 1923.

It would be almost another century before his watermelon landed in a canonical institution. The other, an earlier study of destroyed fruit from 1884, remained in a private collection.

"He was overlooked for so long," Yount said. "There have been surveys of American still life painting over the last decade that didn't include him."

We stepped closer to the canvas.

"I just love how he's created that sense of touch and texture," Yount said. Watermelon "was considered the most challenging of all the still lives, you know, of all the kinds of fruits to paint."

Almost immediately after the Civil War, watermelon was weaponized. With Emancipation, a more formalized type of agricultural entrepreneurship developed for Black Southerners, meaning they could finally draw income from their kitchen garden crops. But what symbolized a path to prosperity for the formerly enslaved blew up as a white supremacist trope in deeply offensive and dehumanizing songs, kitchen gadgets, toys, games, ornaments, postcards, and paintings. By the 1900s, this race shaming was inextricably woven into American popular culture.

The intentionally demeaning stereotype extended to narratives about stealing melons and eating them greedily. The first known American image of Black caricatures exhibiting "an excessive fondness" for watermelon appeared in *Frank Leslie's Illustrated Newspaper* on September 11, 1869. The engraving, made by Confederate veteran and artist William Ludwell Sheppard, was captioned "A Watermelon Feast in Richmond" and showed Black children guzzling fruits. Some of the most derogatory anti-Black artifacts, coinciding with the codification of Jim Crow laws in the South, contained mocking images with bulging eyes and blood-red lips, dark skin and tattered clothing. A young boy, mouth grossly distorted by a whole melon; a little girl in pigtails picking seeds out of a melon, with the caption "He lubs me, he lubs me not." A toothless woman wearing a headscarf, holding an absurdly elongated slice in her hands. The head of a man slowly transmuting into a melon.

The first race-shaming film debuted in 1896, a Vitascope short produced by Edison Studios, titled *Watermelon Eating Contest*, in which two Black men spit fruit at the camera. Nearly a decade later, Edwin S. Porter's silent film *The Watermelon Patch* centered on hungry thieves being smoked out of a cabin by vigilantes with dogs. More deliberately, D.W. Griffith's *Birth of a Nation*, released in 1915, glorified the Ku Klux Klan and villainized free Black citizens; one scene depicted a cartoonish watermelon feast celebrating Emancipation.

Ugly imagery still haunts. After Barack Obama's election, the then-mayor of Los Alamitos, California, sent an email showing watermelons on the White House lawn with the caption: "No Easter egg hunt this year." A syndicated cartoonist for the *Boston Herald* referenced watermelon-flavored toothpaste in a lampoon about an intruder in the 44th president's bathroom. After Disney released *The Princess and the Frog* in 2009, its first animated Black princess was licensed on packaging for watermelon-flavored Dig 'n Dips candy.

Standing in the gallery with Yount and absorbed by the Porter, I nearly missed the painting on the adjacent wall. Only when I turned away did it come into focus.

"Oh my god, it's the Homer."

Winslow Homer painted *The Watermelon Boys* in 1876. Three children—two Black, one white—in a field at the height of summer hold luscious slices. One boy lying on his stomach, bare feet carelessly kicked up, was about to take a bite. A second appeared in close contemplation of his piece. And the boy in the middle, whose facial expression has the most detail, stared off into the distance.

The Met stewards some of the most important Homer works, including *The Veteran in a New Field* from his Civil War period, which also hung in Gallery 762. Embedded with the Union army, Homer reported from the front lines for *Harper's*, sketching battle and camp life scenes. His postwar studies focused on more bucolic subjects and explorations of evolving social norms. Like eating watermelon in "mixed company."

Yount explained that the juxtaposition of Homer's work with Porter's invited conversation about the Black artist's messaging during an era when he might not have been able to speak his truth freely.

"At the time the watermelon subject had become a racist trope, Porter was very intentionally bringing it back to its art historical roots as a symbol of American abundance," she said. "It feels like a more pointed political statement in that cultural context. Reconstruction officially ended in 1877, but . . . we're still living it. Legacy, legacy, legacy. Never resolved."

I took a last good look at the Porter.

He also left one seed clinging to the rind.

DEPRESSION HAM

"How many watermelons did Mose T paint in his lifetime?" I asked.

"Oh my goodness," said Marcia Weber. "Probably more than a thousand? He painted them in all sorts of sizes, but he called the biggest ones Texas watermelons."

A summer street fair had drawn crowds to the riverfront town of Wetumpka, Alabama. Curious visitors distracted Weber with questions about the work on display in her gallery, which specialized in objects by Outsider and self-taught artists such as Howard Finster, Lonnie Holley, and Jimmie Lee Sudduth. The 71-year-old gallerist had originally intended to complete her master's in painting, but in 1981 she accepted a temporary job at the Montgomery Museum of Fine Arts. And then she met Moses Ernest Tolliver, who lived two blocks away, when curators asked her to help with an upcoming exhibition.

"He changed the course of my life," she said.

Born to a family of Alabama sharecroppers around 1920, Tolliver worked as a gardener and handyman to support his family until the late 1960s, when a load of marble slipped off a forklift while he was sweeping the floor at a Montgomery furniture factory. His legs were crushed, and he spent the next couple of years battling depression and drinking heavily. Then Tolliver picked up a brush. From his bed, he covered bits of salvaged furniture, plywood scraps, or Masonite with fanciful flowers, snakes, turtles, dancing ladies, sex workers, and portraits of himself getting around on crutches. He signed his work "Mose T" with a backwards S.

"He told me a red bird was the first thing he painted," Weber said. "And that was on cardboard."

Tolliver would hang paintings in trees and offer them for a few dollars or in trade for snuff to anyone walking past his front porch. More people turned up after a solo show at the Montgomery museum in 1981. Around the same time, he caught the attention of guest curators at the Corcoran Gallery in Washington, DC. The 1982 exhibition, *Black Folk Art in America, 1930-1980*, was a watershed for such self-taught artists as Bill Traylor and Sister Gertrude Morgan. It put Mose T in the same rarified orbit.

In a review of the show, *The New York Times* critic John Russell called their work "uncorrupted art." He wrote: "It was the role of Black folk art to make the unbearable bearable. When all else failed, and society had given the thumbs-down signal once and for all, art was the restorative that made it possible to go on living."

Tolliver and his wife traveled by train to the capital and attended a reception for the show. He met Nancy Reagan. Weber said Tolliver told her that the First Lady acquired two of his paintings for the private White House residence. One of them was a watermelon.

The requests started to pour in.

"Oh, you could not imagine how many letters and notes on fancy, embossed stationery arrived," Weber said. "Most people didn't know where he lived, so they would write care of the museum, and I would go see him every afternoon on my way home."

"So what are the characteristics of a Tolliver watermelon?" I asked.

"Well, normally red was involved, although there would be an occasional yellow watermelon, but those are pretty rare, really. It might have a black rind. I mean, didn't have to have a green rind to be okay for Mose. Often the rind and the seeds might be the same paint. He would use whatever color he had."

Before it came down off the wall and out the front door with new owners, Weber's last Tolliver watermelon was sandwiched between a white-haired self-portrait and a "dyna bird." A fire-hydrant-red melon studded with black seeds, some with specks of white roughly brushed on with quick dabs. A world apart from a Peale, and yet here was the same highlighting technique.

On her desk, Weber kept a framed snapshot of Tolliver sitting side by side with her in the bedroom that doubled as a studio, his denim jeans splattered with the house paint he favored. She admitted that it took time for her to develop an appreciation for Visionary art, but when Weber opened her own gallery in 1991, serious collectors were paying attention to this grassroots genre.

Not all of them were altruistic or fair dealing—questionable contractual arrangements between Black artists and white dealers was the subject of a segment titled "Tin Man" that originally aired on *60 Minutes* in 1993. Trusted sources were crucial for the process, especially with artists whose work was easy to counterfeit or who lacked the ability to read a contract.

Self-taught artists rarely get due respect, and their work may be too quickly judged as childish, one dimensional, or deranged.

"It's been disregarded because it has often been mistaken as an imitation of academically trained fine art," Weber said. "Prior to 1982, it's not been recorded as historically important. So much of it has not survived." Unfortunately, she noted, many of the artists were gone, too.

Tolliver died in 2006 after a bout with pneumonia. His "uncorrupted" paintings were in permanent collections at the Smithsonian, the High Museum in Atlanta, and the American Visionary Art Museum in Baltimore.

Was he intentional about reclaiming watermelon? Collector Scott Blackwell, who produced the documentary *All Rendered Truth: Folk Art in the American South*, also knew Tolliver and would visit him regularly on road trips. "We talked about how much he loved his garden and flowers," he said. "At the end of the day, I'm sure he was well aware of the stigma and prejudice associated with watermelons, but he did sell a ton of melon paintings. and he was never one to shy away from painting what folks wanted to buy."

Around lunchtime, I left Weber to her customers and walked across the street to a hot dog stand. The couple who'd bought the gallery's watermelon painting sat down at the same table. They were up from Montgomery for the day. I asked if they collected folk art, and was told no, but they knew about Tolliver and wanted one of his pieces. Where would they display it?

"Our laundry room," said the wife. "We're going to hang it there."

...

On a wide detour back to Atlanta, I followed a truck on Seedling Drive to the State Farmers Market in Cordele, Georgia. Even if the pickup wasn't piled high with produce, the trail of fruit that smashed on the road was a clear sign that I was entering "The Watermelon Capital of the World" at the height of harvest. (Producers planted between 6,000 and 9,000 acres a year, according to the University of Georgia Extension agent for Crisp County.) Buyers pulled their cars up to the open sheds, where farmers and resellers were loading orders, passing the ripest fruit—both picnic and icebox varieties—hand-to-hand in a high arc.

Picnics are big oblong watermelons, like the one in that Egyptian tomb. Smaller and rounder, iceboxes were engineered to fit in, you guessed it, a fridge. The first seedless specimen was developed in 1939 by Hitoshi Kihara, a geneticist at Kyoto University's Laboratory of Crop Evolution, but they really didn't take off commercially in the States until the 1990s. Now they dominated supermarket sales, although niche varieties like the Bradford, Jubilee, Small Shining Light, and Moon and Stars appeared at roadside stands and wherever melon trucks parked.

"I come at seven o'clock and leave at six," said Roderius "Slim" Jones, who worked every summer at the market since he was thirteen. He lived in Florida but returned to Cordele and stayed with his parents for the season. "I go around and toss watermelons all day."

I chanced a burning question.

"Salt or no salt?"

"It all depends if watermelon is cold or hot," he said. "Watermelon fresh out of the field? No salt. Watermelon cold? Salt."

Salt draws out the sweet and cuts through the bitter. Some of my earliest memories involved a simple summer breakfast of cold watermelon sprinkled with flaky Kosher salt, which my crunchy granola mother introduced during her health food conversion in the 1970s.

"But now I like that Tajín lime salt," Jones said. "I been eating melons all my life but only found out about that stuff this year."

Cordele put me in mind of paintings by Black artist Winfred Rembert, who grew up not far away. One of his most compelling works about farm labor was called *Loading Watermelons* and depicted fieldhands gathering and throwing what looked like Georgia Rattlesnakes into the bed of a truck parked between rows of vines.

Raised by a great-aunt in rural Cuthbert, Georgia, through the early years of the civil rights era, his scenes of life in the segregated Jim Crow South were autobiographical—picking cotton and harvesting melon were common themes—but so were his images of chain gangs.

Rembert was first incarcerated at nineteen after attending an Americus Movement voting rights protest, which took place on the heels of the Selma marches in neighboring Alabama. When he escaped prison in 1967, sheriffs caught and lynched him. Rembert survived, but was forever haunted by the trauma of being hung upside down by his ankles as one of them threatened to emasculate him with a knife. He spent seven more years doing hard labor in the Georgia prison system, and before he was released, Rembert learned how to tool leather from another inmate. Years later, when he was fifty-one, he started carving these narratives into large sheets of leather, using shoe polish as paint, exploring both jubilant and terrible memories. Rembert's genre paintings of pool halls, soda shops, and juke joints in his hometown, and chain gang bosses and inmates in black-and-white prison stripes assigned to roadwork, had the complex energy and bright palette that called to mind similar scenes by social realist Jacob Lawrence.

"Stylistically, his work was about storytelling, not just a moment," said Adam Adelson, when he invited me to view Rembert's *Chopping Watermelon* at his family's gallery in Manhattan. "He had a natural sense of creating compositions, but he figured out perspective on his own. And it wasn't until [later] that his wife said, 'Winfred, you have this amazing life and no one's gonna remember it when you die. You have to tell your story on leather.'"

In *Chopping Watermelon*, workers tended to the vines in diagonal rows. Women in long dresses, men wearing black hats, all carried large hoes. The background was rust orange, like Georgia clay. Rembert wrote that he was fond of Black Diamonds, and several other of his paintings centered on eating them with family. When the Adelsons first gave him a solo exhibition in 2010, they wanted him to document his process. "We had all these pictures and we just sat him down with a notepad and he started writing descriptions of each, and some of them he put on the back of the pictures."

Adelson shared one of these typed statements by Rembert, dated February 1998, about two scenes he painted of people eating slices on a front porch, one simply titled *Watermelon, Saturday Evening*:

"I guess I have to talk about this picture like when I was little before I knew about the stereotype. I don't think I even knew about the stereotype until I was an adult and saw a cartoon showing a Black man caught in a big mousetrap with a watermelon used as bait. Then I understood why white folks used to drive by and stop to take pictures of us eating watermelon. Watermelon was an important part of our socializing, especially on Saturdays and Sundays during watermelon season. The melons would be so thick in the fields, they almost lay on top of each other. We'd get a bunch of them and tie them up in croaker sacks and put the sacks down in the well to cool. Then we'd sit around visiting, jumping rope, playing horseshoes and checkers, and eating watermelon. We always had a real good time."

ESTRELLA

"Get the watermelon margarita," said Rafael Gonzales Jr. His wife, Rozette, ordered oysters and their daughter Presley munched on tortilla chips.

On a Sunday morning in late June, El Bucanero was packed with families sharing gigantic seafood platters. Sharks, squid, and turtles floated on the wall murals; papel picado banners hung from the ceiling. Mariachis roamed from table to table.

San Antonio knew how to brunch.

We first met on social media at the beginning of "La Rona." I followed Gonzales' satirical pandemic series when death and disease monopolized the news because, now and then, the only healthy response was laughter. A Tejano graphic artist and self-proclaimed "piñata rope puller," Gonzales put an image of the virus on a Lotería playing card, the Mexican version of bingo. Corona became La cabRona, a play on the Spanish word for "bitch." The traditional deck had fifty-four pictograms. Rafael and Rozette spent lockdown at their kitchen table putting together an updated edition that captured our collective experience—rolls of toilet paper, hand sanitizer, drive-by birthday parties, relief checks, homeschooling. La Sirena (the mermaid) became a can of tuna fish. El Sol developed a red-hot fever. An ice-cold margarita in a copper Eucharist chalice was La Coping Mechanism. The images went viral.

La Sandía was always an essential Lotería image. It represented abundance, fertility, life and love in Hispanic culture. (One of the earliest mentions of watermelon in a Mexican cookbook dates to 1882.) Gonzales added a picnic melon sliced open on his Lotería's El Food Bank grocery staples card. Another one of his designs featured a large glass jug of watermelon agua fresca.

"Sandía doesn't have the derogatory framings for Hispanics," Gonzales said. "We enjoy it without the stereotypes. In modern culture, watermelon is part of our favorite Mexican snacks. Fruit cups, candies, cocktails."

The global South introduced marvelous ways to eat watermelon, and each culture that arrived in the Deep South expanded the discourse: Vietnamese nước ép dưa hấu, Chinese guazi, Korean subak hwachae, Palestinian bateekh wi jibneh, Indian tarbooz ke chilke ki sabzi, Filipino butong pakwan, Mexican conserva di sandía—all here to stay.

I asked Gonzales to point me to San Antonio's best fruterias, the snack stands that specialized in elaborate fruit cups drizzled with chamoy, tamarind, Tajín, pickle juice, crushed Takis. Fresh squeezed juices, horchatas, mangonadas. Paletas, in rainbow flavors. Gritty raspados

Mexicanos, the acid rock cousin of shaved ice. Nieves, finer ground sno-cones. Anything cold to counter the inexorable heat crushing Texans and their power grid.

After brunch, I drove to El Farolito Refresqueria and Snacks, a lime-green building in a lot near Interstate 35, the main route heading north from the border on the Rio Grande, and one frequently traveled by migrants seeking a new life.

I ordered my new favorite, the Day-Glo watermelon raspado, a sweet-tart ice. I overheat easily and forget to hydrate on long road trips because I don't want to constantly stop for pee breaks. But summer along the Texas-Mexico border could be deadly without water and shade, and the refreshing qualities of watermelon were nowhere more apparent than in a region suffering extended heat dome stress.

Licking fast-melting ice took down the swelter.

JOYRIDE

"Watermelon pops up constantly in my work," said Atlanta-based artist Shanequa Gay. "I see watermelon as sacred, nourishing. It was carried on trips before there were water canisters. It has also long been a negative trope in the Black community alongside fried chicken. Reclamation is key to resistance of oppressed humans."

Gay belonged to a cadre of contemporary artists—Hank Willis Thomas, Kara Walker, Betye Saar, among others—intent on reframing identity and culture. Watermelon was a common symbol for them all.

Slices of picnic melon rested in the arms of the animist spirits Gay called Devouts in her 2020 mural *Sweet Sacrament Divine*, and striped iceboxes appeared among other symbols—cowrie shells, braided hair, black-eyed Susans—representing social protest in the 2021 installation *Her Spirit Will be Our Guide on the Way*. All Saints' Episcopal Church in Atlanta commissioned Gay to interpret the first Station of the Cross, and she chose to render women of color as Christ and Pontius Pilate, who sat in judgment while holding a round watermelon in her lap.

"I was interested in re-contextualizing its meaning as something holy," Gay said. "In Christianity, the Holy Spirit is characterized by water, and so for me, in my work, watermelon symbolizes holiness, histories, the feminine. When the Goddess ran things, Earth was well."

. . .

Gay did the same for problematic portrayals of mythic figures, expressly Disney's offensive animation of "centaurette" Sunflower, a subservient stereotype of a young Black girl that originally appeared in *Fantasia* in 1940. In 1969, the scene was edited for sensitivity, but vintage cutout books containing images of Sunflower chomping watermelon were still out there.

"I look for ways to alter this narrative," Gay said.

The two of us stood in the Skylight Gallery at Oglethorpe University's Museum of Art as her show "thought and memory" floated in a dreamy cosmos. This work—a cobalt blue-and-black mural and paintings of shapeshifters with raven and vulture headdresses—was an exploration of sisterhood. In Gay's personal pantheon, mythic beings—half human, half zebra—represented the power of Black community. (Those centaurettes, ennobled.) Her young girls, thought and memory, wore black-and-white striped stockings and nurtured each other with Kool-Aid, piggybacks, hugs, and naps.

"I did not get to engage with my sister in that way," she admitted.

At heart, she was celebrating rest and play.

"I look at rest as an important aspect in creativity, and we have not had any rest," she said, alluding to the cataclysmic period of pandemic, social upheaval, racial injustice, and an assault on personal freedoms. "When is all of this gonna slow down? You know, can we come to a point of resolution or are we all gonna die while this is going on? What is the legacy of how you contribute to the chaos or fight against the chaos?"

"Nothing is tying your girls down," I said, envious of the otherworldly frolic surrounding us.

I told her about a world championship seed-spitting contest in Texas.

Gay grinned at me.

"Now I'm trying to figure out how I can make my girls spit watermelon. That seems like a superpower to me."

"Spitting seeds is one of my happiest childhood memories," I said.

In my brother Jamie's kitchen hangs a black-and-white photograph taken at our childhood home by my father sometime in the 1960s. Jamie was seated next to our sister Kaki on a rock in the backyard. Both were naked, biting into chunks of watermelon. Little kids, messy eaters. My mother would hose them down afterwards. It remained a treasured family moment.

"My brother told me recently about a game where his friends tried to spit seeds in each other's open mouths," I told Gay. "He said no one cared if they missed and caught one in the eye."

What would summer be without juice on your chin, rinds tossed at your siblings, or seeds launched in the air?

"It is by far the best part of eating a watermelon," Gay said. "I remember sitting on the porch of my great-grandmother and battling my cousins in spitting our seeds. The most barefoot country thing you could do. It felt like freedom."

EXCLAMATION

"Let's go upstairs," said Hilary. "You've got to see this."

After we finished viewing Sarah Miriam Peale's watermelon in the Fogg, I followed my sister up another flight of stairs to the Forbes Pigment Collection. It's off-limits except to art historians and conservators, but a rotating display in cases allowed everyone else to view some of the rarest colors in the archive.

Bitter Egyptian blue, once used to decorate the walls of tombs and temples. The chrome yellow of van Gogh's sunflowers. Vantablack, a carbon nanotube-based paint as dark as a black hole. The geekiest place for two daughters of oil and turps. While neither of us really paints anymore, we remain visual thinkers, and the smell of our father's studio lingers in our dreams.

I bent over the glass to look at a tiny jar of cochineal, the bugs whose crushed bodies produced the bright carmine red color known as Crimson Lake.

The juiciest shade for watermelon.

— Originally published August 2023

Author's Note: The title of this story is taken from Philip Henry Gosse's 1859 account of brutality to enslaved people on a Deep South plantation in his Letters From Alabama, Chiefly Relating to Natural History. *The watermelon has been adopted as a symbol of resistance and solidarity during both Indigenous and international conflicts.*

INFINITE
PETALS

My great-aunt Kathleen Lenore Anderson, everyone called her Kat, was wild for adventure. She drove a cream-colored Cadillac DeVille, one of those late 1960s land yachts that took up more than its fair share of the road, and was not above terrorizing slowpokes on wicked switchbacks in the Great Smoky Mountains outside her home in Knoxville, Tennessee. "Scoot! Scoot! Scoot on down the road," she said, waving her hand imperiously if other drivers didn't pull over and get out of her way. More than once my sister Kaki and I slid sideways across the upholstered backseat. This was long before seat belts were federally mandated, let alone car seats for little girls. To this day, I remember my Nana, Kat's sister, clutching the front dash and admonishing me for dripping chocolate ice cream on the white brocade interior during one particularly furious drift. Aunt Kat just laughed it off.

Lead foot and all, she was probably the most fun of the great-aunts. In her later years, she wore cat's eye glasses, because hilarious. A snappy dresser, rider of camels on retired teacher expeditions, always fast with a joke. An entry in the Winthrop College 1922 yearbook referenced her "attracting much attention for her provincial speech." She had that strong Edisto accent, and shame on those yearbook bitches for their snobbery. In 1936, Kat married a doctor, George Thomas Wilhelm, who served as a professor of preventive medicine at University of Tennessee. Apparently, he was divorced. This was scandalous back then, and for most of her life, my great-aunt referred to a stepson as her "nephew."

She adored my father, her actual nephew, and every Christmas a gift box of Florida citrus would arrive. Oranges, always. Grapefruit, once in a while. Mom, ever frugal, would sneak them into our Christmas stockings for good luck. But it was the kumquats that confounded me as a kid. Coddled in waxed paper, the tiny fruit glowed temptingly like nuggets of gold. (Their Cantonese name, gām gwāt, means golden orange.) Every year, I naively hoped that *this* batch would taste like the juicy navels or Valencias in the same box. And every year, on first bite, the sweet outer skin yielded to puckering disappointment. To be honest, I always thought Aunt Kat was making a cruel joke at my expense, and I gave up on them entirely after those boxes stopped coming, when my dear great-aunt paid off her final speeding ticket and roared past the pearly gates.

GOLDEN COAT

How about a kumquat, my little chickadee?
—W. C. Fields, My Little Chickadee, *1940*

"When my father was 18, he used to load bushels of kumquats on train cars at the depot in San An," said Greg Gude, pointing to a black-and-white photograph from 1948 hanging over his desk at the Kumquat Growers packinghouse on an unpaved cul de sac in Saint Joseph, Florida. "People up North called 'em mini oranges or baby oranges. They were used as ornamentals, most didn't realize you could eat them."

A burly man with curly gray hair, he swiveled in his worn leather chair to remark on more memorabilia in the office. A framed cover story about his father Fred in a local magazine. Brochures featuring a plump cartoon mascot named Katy Kumquat, wearing a billowy chef's hat and spotless white apron. A faded Grand Champion purple ribbon from the 1980 Pasco County Fair for his mother's prized kumquat nut bread. Gude's wife Fanchone fielded calls at another desk crammed behind a playpen for their grandchildren. Among the other jumbles in the office were crayon drawings, Lego toys, Christmas ornaments, empty soda cans. On this cloudless Wednesday morning in late January, the Gudes were prepping for their annual open house, timed with the Dade City Kumquat Festival, when thousands descended on this sleepy farming town among rolling hills west of Orlando.

Their kumquats, courtesy of Aunt Kat, wound up in my Christmas stocking.

Like a lot of native Floridians who still owned a patch of ground wider than a carport, the Gude family grew citrus, mostly as a side hustle to careers in restaurants, military service, and the fire department. (Greg Gude is a retired battalion chief.) His family originally settled outside the hamlet of St. Joe in 1883, when the railroad first came through, which made it easier to ship fruit to distant customers craving a taste of sunshine. Many of his brothers and cousins still live in a tight radius around the original farmhouse, which Gude swore was haunted by a spirit he sometimes spotted in an attic window. His father was born on the property, and his son lived behind the packinghouse on land that belonged to his great-grandfather. After the Great Freeze of 1894 devastated orange groves from Freedtown in Pasco County to the Manatee River, south of Tampa, the family speculated on hardier stock, and that's how they eventually got into kumquats.

"One of my cousins from my mother's side was working in a nursery, and he saw this tree," Gude said. "Nobody really knew the value of it back then [but] he decided to bring one home and plant it. He's what got it rolling into St. Joe." Eventually, Gude's father also took a chance and planted a small block of these novelties alongside his orange grove. So did a neighbor, who harvested oranges for the county's largest frozen concentrated juice plant, and built the original concrete block and tin-roof packinghouse on the shared road. Then, according to Gude, his father received a buyout offer in 1971. "Dad was the father of seven boys, a minimum wage guy working for a gas company, and serving in the National Guard. He had his oranges, but he didn't have a lot of money in hand. He went to four of his friends and asked if they wanted to be in the kumquat business with him."

Greg Gude grabbed a trucker's hat, as Fanchone gathered up recipe cards, and they ambled over to the front door. She turned into the gift shop, where volunteers were arranging jars of kumquat pepper jelly on shelves and laying out bags of kumquat-shaped shortbread cookies on a folding table. I followed her husband through the glare outside, climbed into his UTV, and puttered down the lane to rows of kumquats ready for harvest. The Gudes grew both Nagami and Meiwa varieties. The first had a traditional oval shape; the other was rounder and sweeter. He yanked a few globes off a branch and handed them over. "The Meiwas just don't hold up," he said. "They're very sensitive to cold and heat. If you pick when it's foggy outside, they'll bruise and go bad. I mean, they're just very temperamental, but oddly enough right now they're doing better than the other ones." He explained both varieties grew more like a shrub, and had a curious trait of blooming while fruit still hung heavy. "Kumquats bloom for five months, hence why we can go through and pick them in different stages of the season. And sometimes they will have growth year-round because they're almost ever-bearing."

I got out of the ute for a closer look. Tiny white petals radiated from a yellow pistil. The scent was more delicate and elusive than oranges, requiring close competition with honeybees and fire ants to catch a sniff.

A dump truck roared past at the end of the road and kicked up an entrail of dust.

Gude opened his phone and pulled up a photograph of the family's grove back when mature trees, over 50 years old and 15 feet tall, thrived in tight formation, box-pruned to facilitate harvest. That was before foot rot killed them all in 2015. And then a backdoor freeze in 2018 damaged new trees. Then citrus canker attacked. A farmer sprayed herbicide in an adjoining field and the drift stunted yet another planting.

"There's a lot of drama right there," Gude said. "Welcome to Florida." He started up the ute and headed back to the shed through tall grass.

"I grow the hell out of weeds," he chuckled. "If I could grow kumquats as good, I'd be a millionaire. But still fixing to put in more trees. Keep trying until we can't."

Farmers might be the world's greatest optimists until they stop being farmers.

GOLDEN BULLET

The trees looked haunted, the soul sucked right out of their roots. On a drive the next day between Dade City and Winter Haven, winding through central Florida's biggest commercial citrus groves, which extended for miles on either side of the Orange Blossom Trail, disaster lurched into view as I passed overgrown fields with "for sale" signs, where all hope had surrendered to a perfidious bacteria incongruously known as citrus greening. Also called Huanglongbing, or HLB, this disease is evidenced first as yellowing in leaves, followed by a spreading decline in vigor, the bearing of off-season blooms, and bitter fruit. Then, denuded and dead, down to the ground.

No citrus was immune. All that sunshine in a glass, imperiled.

"This is a citrus tree defender," said Dr. Manjul Dutt, standing next to a sapling draped in a ghostly pillowcase at the Florida Citrus Arboretum. It's one of the experimental methods to ward off HLB—swaddling blocks the sap-sucking psyllids responsible for spreading the pestilence, which arrived in Florida by 2005, and quickly ripped through the state's entire crop. This sheltered grove was a living encyclopedia of all fruits in the *Rutaceae* family. At least, the 250 varieties that thrive in the subtropical Citrus Belt, give or take a few hybridized weirdos exiled to end rows at the back. Possibly Dutt's favorite patch. A horticultural scientist with University of Florida's Citrus Research and Education Center, next door in Lake Alfred, his work was primarily focused on citrus improvement through conventional breeding and biotechnology. Battling HLB was his priority. He was particularly fascinated with fruit that deserves more respect. Like finger limes and kumquats.

"If you were to test these trees, I would say over 95 percent would test positive for the disease."

"That's not good."

"There are some varieties with tolerance from the disease— some varieties of lemons for example—but nothing is bulletproof."

Dutt told me he was born in the Himalayan foothills, 5,000 feet above sea level, in Meghalaya, one of India's far eastern states. Not exactly the right climate for kumquats. "Took me some time to hone my mind to citrus," he said, as we walked between rows of pomelo, etrog, jackfruit, calamansi, and yuzu. "And this tree is very important for India," Dutt said, stopping to pick a fibrous, aromatic, pear-shaped fruit considered sacred to Hindus. "It's called bael."

Both fruit and man, a long way from their homeland.

Dutt's darkened glasses slipped down his nose in the late afternoon humidity. He pushed them back up. "I'm extremely sensitive to bright lights, and I work in Florida," he said, bemused.

The arboretum's collection of kumquats was clustered around an outbuilding, and included *Atalantia hindsii*, also known as the Hong Kong kumquat or golden bean, a wild variety with insignificant, bitter fruit, mainly an ornamental. This dwarf shrub led American botanist Walter T. Swingle to claim in 1914 that kumquats "are the most primitive living true citrous fruits." An ancestor, so to speak, much like the tiny red berries born millennia ago in the Andes that would grow up to become Beefsteaks.

"Kumquats aren't really in the citrus family, right?" I asked.

"Correct. A citrus relative. It's cross compatible," Dutt replied.

"But it's in a class all by its own little oddball self?"

"Fortunella. Its own genus."

The earliest description of kumquats dates to 1178, in *Chü Lu*, a monograph on the oranges of Wên-chou in eastern China, by Sung Dynasty scholar Han Yen-chih. He wrote: "The Chin kan fruit has a golden color, very fine-grained skin, and is considered enjoyable. These fruits are eaten without peeling off their golden coats. When preserved in honey the flavor is still better." In 1699, English privateer and naturalist William Dampier mentioned their general excellence in one of his memoirs, *Voyages and Descriptions*, as compared with other oranges he tasted in the Kingdom of Tonquin (Vietnam). Dampier also reported that "cam-quits" were "accounted very unwholesome fruit, especially to such as are subject to fluxes; for it both creates and heightens that distemper." (Sure, if you ate too many fiber-rich kumquats, they might cause gas, bloating or diarrhea, but scientists had yet to discover that dysentery was caused by poor sanitation and subsequent gut infections, not fruits with golden coats.) Specimens collected on a scientific survey of the Pacific Ocean by the United States Exploring Expedition of 1838–1842—a voyage delightfully nicknamed The Ex. Ex.—finally caught the eye of acquisitive American arborists. Four years later, Robert Fortune, a

Scottish plant hunter, introduced kumquats to Europe. Fortune's name forms the root for their historical classification, but to be honest, botanists were still bickering over kumquat taxonomy.

Being a bastard child was the kumquat's strength. They party like a rock star, producing offspring with incredible new flavor profiles. Specialist purveyors who cater to a small cadre of obsessives (read: big name chefs) were always on the lookout for the next Meyer lemon. Never tasted a Meyer lemon? That's okay. Not everyone is infatuated with the Venn diagram of sweet and tart.

"Do you have any mandarinquats here?" I asked.

Dutt nodded, and we drifted into the back acre, where these curiosities grew. "Here we have some hybrids made with kumquats," he said. "Lemonquats, sunquats, citrangequats, mandarinquats. The Lakeland limequat is a cross between a key lime and a kumquat. The fruit resembles a key lime but has a different flavor."

He picked a ripe one, cut it open with a pocketknife, and squeezed. "Whoa, look at that juice," I said. "Oh, that smells gorgeous." I bit into it. The tart oil lingered for a long time on the tongue. "So do you drink a lot of juice, Dr. Dutt?"

"I like mandarin juice. I'm more of a sweet juice person."

GOLDEN BEAN

"Tampa is coming towards us," Fanchone Gude said, as she walked past the packing line, where Kumquat Growers president Margie Neuhofer was preparing for their first demonstration on Friday morning. "An acre of land is selling for $50,000. Bare land! It's a really big culture shock to all of us who've lived here forever."

"All that development is where I lived," Neuhofer said, adjusting her kumquat bracelet and drop earrings. "My brother-in-law had oranges. We had oranges. And I could go to my carport in my nightgown to get the newspaper. Now I can't because there's homes, you know?"

"Oh, right. You don't want to be running out there in your bathrobe," I said.

"But I mean, we don't do bathrobes," Gude said.

The three of us looked at each other, and cracked up, as only mature women did after blowing past the age of zero F girl.

"Your privacy has gone," Neuhofer said.

She pointed to a 200-acre pasture south of the shed, purchased by a doctor who wanted to sell to a developer who will bulldoze and put up a gated estate community, the kind that attracted pro wrestling stars of the WWE or Buccaneers tight ends looking for tax havens.

"There was a bad freeze in our area and it messed everything up in '83," she said. "By '85, a lot of the people weren't willing to replant. And now if you got a decline, they sell it for homes 'cause the property up here is, they've gone, 'Wow.' But we are still surviving."

"Taking the kids to school today, I passed nineteen dump trucks full of dirt," Gude said.

Both of them worried about what was going to happen to land up the road belonging to an elderly farmer whose sons had no interest in keeping his place going.

"In a state with so many incomers, what does it mean to be a Florida native?" I asked.

"My grandfather's family bought land from the Spanish government," Gude said. "They've been here that long. And if you move here, you should learn to live here, not want to change everything."

On most days, the only people parked under the "Welcome to Saint Joseph, The Kumquat Capital" sign on the side of the packinghouse were delivering rootstock or picking up frozen pulp headed to a processor making kumquat jam and chutney. But once a year, when neighboring Dade City overflowed during the

Kumquat Festival, customers detoured down Gude Road to buy Mother Rosemary's famous kumquat "refrigerator" pie. A part-time employee now bakes the pies, but Greg's mother developed the original recipe, a creamy concoction held together with condensed milk and Cool Whip.

Out on the lawn, a guitarist finger-plinked the national anthem. A cousin poured his home-brewed kumquat beer and the Knights of Columbus grilled hot dogs with pickled kumquat chutney. Greg Gude hitched a trolley to his tractor and hauled visitors around the grove, as his harvester Tony Dejada snapped Meiwa kumquats off branches with a flick of his wrist, then plopped them in a plastic bucket strapped across his shoulder. He and his wife Margie started picking for Kumquat Growers in 1972. Before the freezes and diseases knocked them back, the cooperative harvested up to 18,000 bushels a year. Now, after a drought year, it was down to about 1,000, so the Dejadas worked alone for the most part, with a rhythm all their own.

The trolley turned a corner at the far end of the grove and deposited passengers at a back door so they could watch fruit tumbling down a conveyor belt. Rural packinghouses were always an essential way station between field and regional markets—several Florida citrus sheds have been listed in the National Register of Historic Places. But compared to commercial facilities for processing oranges, this shed was minuscule, with a single line operated by five seasonal workers who sanitized, sorted, and loaded kumquats into vented clamshells.

Fanchone Gude greeted the crowd after they found seats on benches against the walls. She passed out kumquats, and then asked how many had ever eaten one before.

I spotted another lady who had already mangled hers, the outer skin peeled down like a tangerine, with the pulp exposed.

Fanchone changed that.

"Hold it between your fingers and squeeze until the oil sprays out," she said. "Then put it in your mouth and chew, chew, chew. It's two different flavors and you can't duplicate that."

The sensation reminded me of those sweet-tart candies sold in dollar stores. Still an acquired taste, but a happier medium.

Greg Gude chimed in.

"You can even swallow the seeds," he said. "They expand and curb your appetite. We have one study that said this would help you lose weight."

His wife shot back.

"Um, are you looking at me 'cause I haven't?"

GOLDEN HEART

"Kadence had to do her SATs this morning at the high school," said Courtney Loss, Dade City's kumquat pageant director, about her title winner. "I told her you've got the luck of the kumquat behind you, just breathe, take your time."

Loss was on her phone trying to locate Miss Kumquat, who was stuck in traffic after her test. She suffered from a degenerative neuropathy in her hands and struggled to tap the screen. It was Saturday morning, right before the Kumquat Festival kickoff.

The kumquat court was getting bored waiting. Little girls wearing embroidered sashes and tiaras jumped up and down on the stone seating outside the county courthouse. Tiny Miss Kumquat sat on the ground with her crayons to finish coloring in a cartoon handout. Wee Mister and Young Mister reached for coins in the fountain. Baby Miss needed a diaper change. Loss handed out "Kumquat Royalty" T-shirts.

"So do you have a queen or princess?" I asked.

"Well, Miss Kumquat is essentially our queen."

For a long time, Pasco County had no kumquat queen. Loss' mother organized the first pageant a quarter century earlier, when the chamber of commerce launched a festival to promote local growers like the Gudes and Neuhofers. Back then, Dade

City was buffered from the loom of Orlando by the Green Swamp Wilderness Preserve. As subdivisions encroached along Interstate 75, the city clung to a certain nostalgia for its "cracker cowboy" past. Floridians claimed this uncomfortable term as a mark of their frontier heritage, breathlessly suggesting it first emerged because cattlemen cracked bullwhips to herd the criollo cows introduced by Spanish explorers like Panfilo de Narvaez, who trudged through here in May 1528.

No one wanted to talk about other uses for those whips.

Police cruisers began to block off traffic to downtown, where vendors were setting up to sell kumquat ice cream, tea towels, trucker hats, balloons, margaritas, and even kumquat-flavored meatballs to the expected crowd of 30,000 snowbirds. Storefronts competed for best kumquat window decorations. The Sacred Heart Early Childhood Center sliced pies donated by Kumquat Growers at their booth, while several blocks away Greg Gude roped off a pathway to displays filled with netted bundles of fruit from the shed.

Loss explained her mother gave up the pageant because it got to be too much for one person to manage. Not just the competition but also all the events to attend, the sponsorship money to hustle, and the outfits to order.

"I talked to Greg Gude and I was like, 'Hey, what do you think about bringing Miss Kumquat back?' And he's like, 'Absolutely.' So last year was my first group of girls and this is my second."

"Where did you get their crowns?"

"I ordered them online. What's great is you can buy them in bulk and they do matching sets."

Tiny Miss, whose name is Melanie Hermon, finished her crayon drawing. The 5-year-old handed it to her mother and marched off with the other girls and boys for a photo session on the courthouse lawn. Dressed in bell-bottom jeans and leopard print cowboy boots, her fawn brown hair tangled in a tiny tiara.

"Is this her first pageant?" I asked.

Her mother, Jamie, shook her head no.

"We entered her in a different one last year and then she asked every weekend if there was a pageant, and I was like, 'Oh my gosh.' So then when we heard about this one, she was all excited."

"Do you think you'll do it again?"

"Melanie gave a speech during the pageant and we still hear it every day. She loves to be on stage."

"Some people have that talent," I said.

Rising to follow her daughter, Hermon grabbed up a backpack.

"Yeah. I'm not one for the stage, but she's the polar opposite. She loves it. The bigger the crowd, the more excited she is, and I'm like, 'Oh, not me.'"

. . .

Courtney Loss buttonholed the mayor, James D. Shive, as he stepped out of the courthouse to greet festival goers. He wore running shorts and a creamsicle-orange shirt pinned with an official name tag that read "Proud Heritage, Promising Future."

"Hi, Mr. Shive."

"How are you?" he said, shaking her hand. "Good to see y'all. What beautiful young ladies."

The mayor bent over Baby Miss, toddling perilously toward the edge of a bench.

"What a prime example here," he said.

Shive looked up again as Loss threw her pitch.

"We want to look into what we have to do to start a kumquat parade. Like on Friday night?"

The mayor nodded along. He probably nodded along a lot.

"The open house out at Kumquat Growers ends at three, so a five-thirty or six o'clock kind of thing. And maybe it could grow, but something that would be an extra showcase."

Shive's assistant appeared, hovering.

"We'll get with you," he said vaguely, waving to the pageant parents.

Florida has a long history of citrus parades. And counter-parades. During the late 1980s, the Queen Kumquat Sashay in Orlando was billed as the "Parade for People Who Would Not Be Permitted in Any Other Parade." It was a tribute to the absurd and the raunchy. The first grand marshal was a 2.4-inch Madagascar hissing cockroach. Off-duty Walt Disney World musicians formed the World's Worst Marching Band while dancers from Thee Dollhouse, a strip club on Orange Blossom Trail, threw condoms to the crowd from the back of a pickup truck. Other parade marchers tossed kumquats, only to have the little bombs thrown back at them. Any woman with red hair—drag queens welcome—could be crowned Kumquat Queen if they showed up when the parade began. Festival founder Bob Morris was blindfolded, as the redheads surrounded him, and in a twisted version of "pin the tail," a random winner would be whisked away in a kumquat-orange VW Karmann Ghia.

Perhaps Dade City could bring the joy to its kumquat parade as well.

GOLDEN COIN

On the way out of Dade City, I stopped back at Kumquat Growers one last time to buy a pie for friends living down the coast. The road quickly emptied of traffic and solitary cows grazed on bales of hay. As usual, I managed to park in the exact wrong spot and stepped on a fire ant whose sisters took their revenge on my bare ankles. Greg Gude had told me he loves fire ants, because they will take down pesky insects looking to invade his grove, so I guess it was my own fault for not wearing sturdier shoes.

Fanchone Gude stood alone in the gift shop, restocking shelves with kumquat honey and hot sauce. She sold me a pie and gave me a bag of ripe Nagamis to take home as well. As she picked up a "Buy Fresh" sign, Edward "Ed" Blommel, a regional director for the Florida Department of Agriculture, walked in. Gude knows him as Eddie, because naturally, he grew up around the corner. "You know how you're introduced to someone and you call them something for the rest of their life?" she laughed.

They chatted about bingo nights and spaghetti dinners at Saint Mary's Episcopal. Then Blommel pulled a gold coin out of his pocket and handed it to her.

"You all are a credit to the state of Florida," he said.

Gude blushed.

On one side, the coin depicted a grove of citrus under a rising run. The flip side was embossed with the Office of Agricultural Law Enforcement seal. "The commissioner has this challenge coin," Blommel said. "It's for people in agriculture. And the challenge is that we want them to stay in agriculture."

"Greg has always wanted one of these," Gude said. "Our granddaughter already got one."

"And now so do you."

"He's going to be so jealous."

Blommel grinned and gave her a second one.

"Give me a call about bingo. We never win but Libby and I love to play."

Several hours later, Greg Gude parked his truck behind the packinghouse, where his wife found him rummaging between the front seats, frazzled after a long day.

"Fanchone, did you see where my gun is at? I can't find it," he said.

She looked startled, glanced at me, then shrugged. "We've been through a lot this year," she said.

Gude sighed after discovering his weapon had slipped underneath the cup holder. He stuffed the holster in the back waistband of his pants and pulled his shirt over it.

"Eddie Blommel was here, and he missed you," she said.

"Sorry about that."

"But he left you this."

She handed him the challenge coin, and her husband held it gingerly in his palm, pride rolling across his tired face.

"Oh wow. Just . . . just wow."

GOLDEN FORTUNE

A few years ago, I realized sweets were no longer as tempting as that ice cream cone in the back of my great-aunt's Cadillac. I could push past the racks of candy bars at supermarket checkout lines, stop ordering desserts at restaurants, and give up soda. Okay, that's a lie, because Coke and boiled peanuts. For whatever reason, the bitter center of kumquats no longer disappointed, and appealed more than the sweet peel. This brings to mind the *Urban Dictionary* definition of kumquat: "A young individual who goes through life constantly disappointing people with his/ her infinite failures."

After returning home from Florida, I pickled the Gudes' always blooming Nagamis. Maybe it's an aging palate. Or just age. I've nearly hit that same stage of life as Aunt Kat when she drove us to Nashville to see the Grand Ole Opry perform at the Ryman Auditorium, and bought me a pretty turquoise ring shaped like a flower at a cheesy trading post in Gatlinburg. My Nana was convinced that cheap silver ring would fall apart, and for the rest of the trip I held my thumb down on the petals for fear they would pop out of their setting. I still have that ring, all these years later, and hope to forever.

— Originally published September 2024

SHATTER
POD

"Have another cookie," said Gertrude, passing me a Tupperware bowl as we sat on the porch at her beach house. After an unsettling night in a place that should have felt like a homecoming, I turned up on her doorstep, almost a stranger, but she invited me to stay anyway. Gertrude Julia Bailey Woods was a distant cousin of sorts, with blood ties in the manner of most relationships on Edisto, where an old family tree might repeat the same names over and over in ascending, entangled branches. Gertrude was also my great-aunt Lila Jean's childhood best friend, and they rode horses together to a one-room schoolhouse on the island's unpaved roads.

After retirement, Gertrude volunteered with the sea turtle watch, walking the Atlantic dunes across from her house to spot endangered loggerheads during nesting season. One of her life dreams was to see a puffin in the wild. She taught Sunday school at Trinity Episcopal and contributed recipes to its community cookbook. Took me down paths I never would have found on my own. Told me stories that I have since passed along. Hands down, of all my relatives, she made the best benne cookies, so brittle and crunchy, as thin as a blade of sweetgrass, with an elusive flavor Gertrude attributed to a secret ingredient. On that first trip back to Edisto as a young adult, I ate them every afternoon.

For some, the seeds represent good luck.

OPEN SESAME

Benne arrived on our shores in the holds of slave ships, carried by men and women who lost everything except a handful of lucky seeds, kept secret in a pocket, a hem, a braid of hair. It's called benne in the Carolina Lowcountry, rather than sesame, because the Gullah word is derived from běne, a term in the Malinké trade language, spoken throughout the West Africa countries linked to the Middle Passage. The spelling "benny" was first mentioned on this side of the Atlantic in a *Georgia Gazette* article on May 25, 1774, but it was already planted by enslaved people in their own modest kitchen gardens as early as the seventeenth century, and would also appear in one of the South's grandest kitchen gardens because Thomas Jefferson was a fool for salad oil.

Sesamum indicum was considered one of the world's oldest known oilseed crops, and thanks to a bottle gifted from one of Jefferson's botanical correspondents, an experimental farmer and politician named William Few, the third president first tasted sesame oil at the White House in 1808. He wrote back to Few about its superiority to imported olive oil: "I would prefer to have it fresh from my own fields to the other brought across the Atlantic and exposed in hot warehouses."

Shortly after, Jefferson sent seed to his granddaughter, Anne Cary Randolph, with instructions to his enslaved gardener Wormley Hughes to sow it in "some open place" in the vegetable patch at Monticello. On April 29, 1809, Jefferson noted in his meticulous garden book the second attempt at planting "Benni, from Bailey's walk to Stable yard." He would persist with this "oily grain" experiment on and off for the next fourteen years, and while Jefferson occasionally dabbled in the dirt, he wasn't the one regularly hefting a hoe in the row.

Born in March 1781, Wormley Hughes was the son of Betty Brown, a half-sister to Sally and James Hemings, and from the age of 13, he pounded out nails with other enslaved boys on Mulberry Row, the property's industrial quarters, and then most likely apprenticed with Robert Bailey, the Scottish gardener hired by Jefferson to lay out the grounds on the mountaintop plantation outside Charlottesville, Virginia. After Bailey's tenure, Hughes eventually became principal gardener, in charge of seed propagation, and was mentioned frequently in Jefferson's horticulture records and correspondence. Because of this we know he loved horses, planted trees, spread manure on the vegetables, tended the extensive flowerbeds, and, while not formally freed in the end, was "given his time." His wife and children, however, were sold away.

Hughes would also dig Jefferson's grave.

On a dew-heavy morning, I walked the vegetable garden with Peggy Cornett, Monticello's Curator of Plants. Of the many times I've visited the grounds, it was the first I'd seen Jefferson's botanical laboratory in bloom, where he grew 89 different species and 330 varieties of vegetables and herbs, not all destined for the table. Hewn from a mountain slope and supported by a massive stone wall, the two-acre terrace overlooked an orchard, vineyard, and berry plots.

"We're facing south?" I asked.

"South southeast," Cornett said. "It's exposed, and not shaded, so it's a hot garden."

"And this is where the benne was planted?"

"In the orchard," she said, indicating the meadow downhill. "On the other side of the vineyard. They were trying to plant large quantities of it, not just a row in the vegetable garden."

"I understood Jefferson used it to box in his carrots."

"One of his squares was lined with sesame. One year. Not every year."

We crunched along the red clay path surrounding the plots, past salsify, white mustard, lettuces, a bean arbor.

"I found a variety of sesame called Monticello White in an online seed catalog."

"They call it Monticello?" Cornett asked. She snorted. "We don't have any Monticello sesame."

"So is that just total bullshit?"

"Yeah. People do that a lot," Cornett said. "I don't know where we got our seed from originally, but it wasn't passed down from Thomas Jefferson or any of the enslaved."

Cornett, who had degrees in botany and ornamental horticulture, managed the grounds at another plantation with a complicated history—Oak Alley in Louisiana—before arriving at Monticello in 1983. She was mindful of her unpaid, less acknowledged predecessors. "Jefferson's granddaughters would mention Wormley in their letters. You know, 'Wormley's gonna do this,' and then Jefferson would say, 'Well, Wormley will know what to do with those trees. He'll know where to plant them.' He was in his twenties when Jefferson retired in 1809, and he was always digging."

We paused next to the restored garden pavilion where Jefferson spent summer evenings reading. Michael Tricomi, Curator of Historic Gardens, walked up from the orchard.

"Are you planting benne soon?" I asked. "What's your season for it here?"

"Usually late spring, early summer to late fall," he said.

"Does it need anything?"

"It likes warmth." He smiled. "We usually let it just totally go to seed and leave the stalks in the garden until you gotta get it at the right time, because you don't want seeds scattering everywhere."

Tricomi is only one of many heritage gardeners to recognize the particular task of harvesting these pods. Braiding Seeds fellow Amirah Mitchell stewards seeds fundamental to African diaspora foodways at her farm outside Philadelphia—she refers to benne as a joyful harvest, for her own pleasure, because the seeds sound like a rainmaker instrument as they spill out when clipped from their stalks.

Cornett and I ended our walk at the Contemplative Site, a 60-foot-long steel memorial pierced with the names of 607 men, women, and children enslaved at Monticello, in an area Jefferson once called the Grove. Wormley Hughes appeared halfway along the panel. Apparently, he was often heard to remark: "I am in no wise discouraged."

Before leaving, I drove Cornett back down the mountain to Tufton Farm, one of Monticello's original outlying "quarter" farms, now the Thomas Jefferson Center for Historic Plants. She guided me through the nursery into a refrigerated container that serves as the seed bank, pulled a packet off a shelf, and handed it to me.

OILY GRAIN

"So I'm gonna make some candy for you," said Christina Miller. Standing at a stovetop in a North Charleston ghost kitchen, as other cooks and caterers worked furiously to load hot boxes headed to private parties on the peninsula, the young owner of a soul bakery and ice cream truck measured sugar into a large saucepan full of melted butter. "Traditionally, you would have used cane syrup for the benne candy," she said. "You need some sort of fat, so I use butter, and then the benne seeds, and that's literally it."

Where some see salad oil, others see sweets.

One of the earliest mentions of benne candy appears in Emily Wharton Sinkler's personal receipt book, which she started in 1855. Originally from Philadelphia, she married into a family of planters and resided at properties named Belvidere and The

Eutaw in Upper Saint John's Parish, which are now submerged under the waters of Lake Moultrie. Sinkler would have become familiar with this treat during her time in Charleston, where elderly female street hucksters also sold groundnut cakes, coconut "monkey meat," and sweet potato pone. Sinkler most likely patronized freeborn pastry chef and restaurateur Eliza Seymour Lee, who inherited her formerly enslaved mother's bakery and catering business, and delighted customers with teacakes, hot buns, pies, and jellies, until she retired in 1861.

Candies were peddled on the street until 1909, when the city passed a sanitation regulation known as the Fly Ordinance, effectively ending the trade. "People were still making 'em in their homes though," Miller said as she poured benne into the pan. "You would share it amongst your family if you had benne plants in your backyard. And now there's a resurgence of that kind of stuff. Before my food truck, I sold at the farmers market in Marion Square, and the first time I took the candy out, you would not believe how many people—mainly African American—were like, 'Oh my God, I have not had this candy since I was a child.'"

When she turned four, Miller learned how to roll pie dough and fill cake pans in the kitchens of her two grandmothers, Bertha and Eutellia, so she named her bakery Bert & T's Desserts in their honor. A registered nurse, Miller specialized in the old school Gullah Geechee treats like chewies, jelly cakes, rice pie, sweet potato bread pudding, and benne brittle.

Miller swirled vanilla into her batter. "I like vanilla in my candy," she said. "We're kind of spoiled by commercial candy. It's our reference point for things, but just so you know, it was sometimes flavored with lemon peel or orange peel."

"Do you toast the seeds?" I asked.

"When I do benne ice cream, and sometimes cookies, I find that toasting them helps to intensify the flavor. But it's really not necessary in the candy."

The pot started to bubble, and Miller stirred constantly as the mix caramelized. Someone at another station dropped sheet pans with a loud crash, and we both looked up, but she quickly turned back to the saucepan.

"This is so easy to burn when it gets to this stage," she said. "You can't even walk away from it."

Miller told me she sourced locally grown benne by the pound from the GrowFood Carolina warehouse in Charleston and the Gullah Farmers Cooperative on St. Helena Island. When her candy reached the soft crack stage, Miller pulled it off the stove and moved to a prep table where she had a sheet pan lined with parchment paper. She poured it out, swiftly spread the candy in a thin layer, scored it with a knife, and then peeled glossy pieces off the paper.

"I have a really good friend that's Nigerian," she said. "He came over to the States when he was eleven. And he's like, 'We make this candy too!' And they do the same down in the Caribbean. It's just crazy to see how the diaspora and foodways are so connected."

Nigerian kantun ridi.

Puerto Rican dulce de ajonjolí, Bahamian benny cakes, Belizean wangla.

I popped a piece of the brittle in my mouth. It was delicately nutty, still a bit chewy and warm, the right degree of sweet without being cloying. "This is so much better than the stale wafers that came in those touristy tins," I said, reminded of a failed confectionery that once occupied the Old Slave Mart on Chalmers Street.

Miller beamed. "People keep sharing recipes with me because they know what I'm doing. And for me, that's like gold."

CLOSE SESAME

Cookie Monster was one of my favorite characters on *Sesame Street*. He debuted on November 10, 1969 in the show's first episode, and while he grew famous for an insatiable craving, I came to appreciate this wise crumb shared by a blue puppet with googly eyes: "Me no cry because cookie is finished. Me smile because cookie happened."

My cousin Gertrude was like that, too. She never saw a puffin in the wild, but she gave me a sea turtle carving as a wedding gift. A year later, in 1995, her sons called to say that she died on the operating table during hip replacement surgery. My great-aunt Lila Jean, who gave me a painting of the Edisto marsh by her older brother, my grandfather, followed her friend months later. That silenced a generation who grew up before the bridge, between hurricanes, trading penny candy from rival island stores. The painting hung in my dining room, the turtle on a bookshelf. The best gift of all was an index card. Gertrude typed out her recipe for extra thin benne cookies, sharing her secret ingredient at last, and included the following instructions:

"Bake in a 350 degree oven until brown. Watch carefully. Don't get involved in telephone conversation or engrossed in TV program . . . When cookies have cooled, they slide right off the foil. No tears or regrets."

How lucky to have spent even a few summer visits in the kitchen of this kind woman. Benne will not thrive where I live now, in the unsympathetic cold of northernmost New York, so I opened the packet Peggy Cornett shared from Monticello and added the tiny white seeds to a batch. At the end of a meal, there should always be a cookie like Gertrude's.

No tears, no regrets.

— September 2024

SHATTER POD

A list of literary works that enriched *The Crop Cycle*

A Carolina Rice Plantation of the Fifties by Alice R. Huger Smith

A Diary from Dixie by Mary Boykin Chesnut

"A Dish of Peaches in Russia" by Wallace Stevens

"A Meeting" by Wendell Berry

A Member of the Wedding by Carson McCullers

American Cookery by Amelia Simmons

An Hour Before Daylight by Jimmy Carter

"As I am Dying" by Alice Walker

Beloved by Toni Morrison

Blue Grass Cook Book by Minnie C. Fox

Cane by Jean Toomer

Charleston Receipts by Junior League of Charleston

COMBEE: Harriet Tubman, the Combahee River Raid, and Black Freedom During the Civil War by Edda Fields-Black

"Cyclewali" by Naazeen Diwan

Fried Green Tomatoes at the Whistle Stop Cafe by Fannie Flagg

From Okra to Greens: A Difference Love Story by Ntozake Shange

God, Dr. Buzzard, and the Bolito Man: A Saltwater Geechee Talks About Life on Sapelo Island by Cornelia Walker Bailey

Good Old Grits by Bill Neal

Gullah Spirit: The Art of Jonathan Green

Journal of a Residence on a Georgian Plantation, 1838-1839 by Frances Anne Kemble

Iron Pots & Wooden Spoons by Jessica Harris

La Cuisine Creole by Lafcadio Hearn

"Land:Bone/Ocean:Muscle" by Sneha Subramanian Kanta

Letters From Alabama Chiefly Relating to Natural History by Philip Henry Gosse

Longthroat Memoirs: Soup, Sex, and Nigerian Taste Buds by Yemisi Aribisala

"My Ancestor Was an Ancient Astronaut" by Toba Beta

Mrs. Hill's New Cook Book by Annabella P. Hill

'night, Mother by Marsha Norman

Oranges by John McPhee

"Peach Blossom Spring" by Tao Yuanming

"Pity for Poor Africans" by William Cowper

Sugar Changed the World by Marc Aronson and Marina Budhos

"Surrender" by Jacqueline Kolosov

Sweetness and Power by Sidney W. Mintz

The African Heritage Cookbook by Helen Mendes

The Carolina Housewife by Sarah Rutledge

The Carolina Rice Kitchen by Karen Hess

The Georgia Peach by William Thomas Okie

The Jemima Code by Toni Tipton-Martin

The Kentucky Housewife by Lettice Bryan

The Piano Lesson by August Wilson

The Picayune's Creole Cookbook

The Prince of Tides by Pat Conroy

The Savannah Cookbook by Harriet Ross Colquitt

The Virginia House-wife by Mary Randolph

Tomatoland: How Modern Industrial Agriculture Destroyed Our Most Alluring Fruit by Barry Estabrook

Vibration Cooking, or The Travel Notes of a Geechee Girl by Vertamae Smart-Grosvenor

"Watermelons" by Charles Simic

Within the Plantation Household: Black and White Women of the Old South by Elizabeth Fox-Genovese

White Trash Cooking by Ernest Matthew Mickler

"Woman Poem" by Nikki Giovanni

ACKNOWLEDGMENTS

One of the defining aspects of my childhood was the creative vortex swirling around our small town in upstate New York, where my parents belonged to a cadre of artists, musicians, writers, actors, and filmmakers, all exiles from elsewhere, mostly Manhattan, that feral realm of agents, editors, and gallerists, who they ignored until the bills piled up. This generation threw wacky parties, traded art and vinyl, pranked each other relentlessly, and hung truly odd crap in their studios, including taxidermy birds and a store window mannequin. (We named her Martha, as in Martha Mitchell, the summer of the Watergate hearings.) They raised oddball pets and even odder kids. And like all good things, it came to an end, as one by one, everyone moved on.

I jealously desired that same kind of collective energy, which eluded me for a long time, until Kyle Tibbs Jones, one of the founders of *The Bitter Southerner*, sent me a message after I liked a social media post about mariachis in Atlanta. It led to an assignment that tapped into my storytelling reserves about family, history, food, and the South. The pay? A T-shirt and a shot of whiskey. Since then, Team BS has introduced me to another vortex of talented human beings, all connected to making art out of a common heritage. What a thrill to be caught up in that, because they don't mind my truly odd crap either.

Mercy buckets to Kyle Tibbs Jones, Dave Whitling, and Eric NeSmith. Equal thanks to all the editors who toiled on each of these stories. Jan Winburn, especially. Alison Law, for herding them into this anthology. Here's to the many incredible photographers who showed up in the buggy fields or hot kitchens, translated when my basic Spanish failed to catch crucial nuances, and shared meals on long drives into the boonies. Amanda Greene, Audra Melton de Elgarrista, Fernando Decillis, Greg Dupree, Growl (Chris McClure and Justin Weaver), Johnny Autry, Josh Letchworth, Michael Cirlos, Rinne Allen, Tammy Mercure. A special bow to the extraordinary artist Shanequa Gay, who shares a continuing dialogue with me about powerful women, real and imagined. Cheers to the people who fed me on the way, or offered a bed at the end of the day. Wendell Brock and Miss Shirley in Atlanta. My cousins Ann Kulze, Becky Baird, Etta Connolly, and Harry Gregorie in Charleston. Their sister Dicksie, miss your wicked grin. Their mother, Jane. Simone Rathle in New Orleans. Larry and Jo Ann Golden in Bonita Springs. Marlee and A. D. Hart in Charlottesville. Rikki and Mike Skopp in Siloam Springs. Matthew and Jenny McClure in Bentonville. Ethan Eang Lim in Chicago. Diego Galicia, Rico Torres, Esaul and Anais Ramos in San Antonio.

Research and sources are vital to any journalist, and I've been fortunate to have most people open their doors when I turn up asking difficult questions. The Immigrant Justice Project at Southern Poverty Law Center was core to reporting on onions, the Coalition of Immokalee Workers on tomatoes. The Marlene and Nathan Addlestone Library Special Collections at College of Charleston. The South Carolina Historical Cookbooks Collection at University of South Carolina Libraries. The Lupton African American Cookbook Collection at the University of Alabama. The Lowcountry Digital Library. Lowcountry Africana. The Southern Food and Beverage Museum and the Historic New Orleans Collection at the Williams Research Center. Thomas Jefferson Center for Historic Plants at Monticello. The National Museum of African American History and

Culture, and the National Museum of the American Indian, both at The Smithsonian Institution. The Metropolitan Museum of Art, the Fogg Museum at Harvard University, Crystal Bridges Museum of American Art, The Gibbes Museum of Art, The Oglethorpe University Museum of Art. Matt Sartwell at Kitchen Arts & Letters in New York and Celia Sack at Omnivore Books in San Francisco for digging through their rare titles and offering me peeks at books I couldn't afford to buy.

For every one of my family, still here or jolted beyond. Mom and Dad, who never really returned South for good, barring that final ride. My sisters and brother, Kaki, Jamie, Melissa, Hilary. The next generation, Jameson, Kate, Kaki, and Shane, when they get around to asking questions about where they come from. Our uncles, on both sides. Nana and her sisters, the greatest aunts of all time. And my grandfather, who went before I was born, but left behind photo albums that drew me back to his island.

Bronson Hager, my husband, my plot device.

Still owed that shot of whiskey.

Shane Mitchell writes narrative nonfiction and cultural criticism. She is the recipient of five James Beard Foundation awards, including two M.F.K. Fisher Distinguished Writing prizes, for her stories on consequential crops and problematic food histories. While she lives in northern New York, both sides of her family are deeply rooted in the rural South. Her father's ancestors were Huguenot refugees who arrived in South Carolina in the late seventeenth century, while her mother's relatives settled in western Tennessee soon after. Some of them may have distilled moonshine, but no one is saying for sure. Shane challenges systemic Southern cultural bias without reservation, but also finds joy in the eccentric rituals of the region. She still hates grits.